BUILDING A SUSTAINA...
A RAND Project to Explore U. ...ging World

Russian Views
OF THE
International
Order

Andrew Radin
Clint Reach

Prepared for the Office of Net Assessment, Office of the Secretary of Defense

For more information on this publication, visit www.rand.org/t/RR1826

Library of Congress Cataloging-in-Publication Data is available for this publication.
ISBN: 978-0-8330-9727-9

Published by the RAND Corporation, Santa Monica, Calif.
© Copyright 2017 RAND Corporation
RAND® is a registered trademark.

Cover: Kremlin by yulenochekk/Fotolia; map by Naeblys/Fotolia.

Support RAND
Make a tax-deductible charitable contribution at
www.rand.org/giving/contribute

www.rand.org

Preface

Since the end of the Cold War, Russian officials and analysts have expressed increasingly harsh views of the U.S.-led international order. Although Russia initially sought to integrate into the Western system in the early 1990s, Russia's leaders today view the U.S.-led order as a threat to Russia's core interests in its perceived sphere of influence. This report analyzes Russian views of the U.S.-led international order by identifying Russian interests, perspectives on order, and policies toward key components of order. The goal is to identify key points where Russian and U.S. views of the international order conflict, thereby highlighting the trade-offs, risks, and opportunities in pursuing or compromising the U.S. vision of the international order.

This report is part of Building a Sustainable International Order, a larger RAND Corporation project that seeks to understand the existing international order, assess current challenges to the order, and recommend future U.S. policies with respect to the order. For more information on the project, visit www.rand.org/nsrd/projects/international-order.

Human subjects protection protocols have been used in this research in accordance with the appropriate statutes and U.S. Department of Defense regulations governing human subjects protections. The views of sources rendered anonymous by such protocols are solely those of the sources and do not represent the official policy of the U.S. Department of Defense or the U.S. government.

This research was sponsored by the Office of the Secretary of Defense's Office of Net Assessment and conducted within the International Security and Defense Policy Center of the RAND National Defense Research Institute, a federally funded research and development center sponsored by the Office of the Secretary of Defense, the Joint Staff, the Unified Combatant Commands, the Navy, the Marine Corps, the defense agencies, and the defense Intelligence Community.

For more information on the International Security and Defense Policy Center, see www.rand.org/nsrd/ndri/centers/isdp or contact the director (contact information is provided on the web page).

Contents

Figures

Summary

U.S. officials and analysts have identified increasing pressure on the existing U.S.-led international order, especially from Russian aggression in Ukraine. With the goal of informing possible U.S. policy options for revising or strengthening the current international order, this report examines Russian views of the international order. In short, Russian leaders and analysts see the current international order as dominated by the United States and as a threat to Russian interests and security. Although Russia has sought to undermine elements of the current international order that it sees as particularly threatening, there are several areas where U.S. and Russian interests overlap and cooperation is feasible.

This report describes Russian views of the current international order, drawing from analysis of Russian interests and Russian views of the history of the post–Cold War period. Russia's underlying foreign policy interests have remained relatively consistent since the end of the Cold War. These interests include maintaining Russia's territorial integrity, preserving the regime, exercising dominance within Russia's "near abroad" (meaning Russia's perceived sphere of influence, which Russian analysts characterize as the former Soviet Union minus the Baltic states), securing noninterference in domestic affairs as a fundamental principle of global governance, and pursuing political and economic cooperation as a partner equal to other great powers.

Russian leaders and analysts contend that Russia sought integration into Western institutions in the 1990s. However, Russia's effort to more closely join the U.S.-led order was not successful, in these people's view, because the West would not recognize Russia's interests. Russian officials and analysts began to perceive the U.S.-led order as increasingly threatening following Western military operations in Bosnia and Herzegovina, Kosovo, and Iraq and because of the perceived U.S. facilitation of "color revolutions."[1] Over time, Russia began to lose interest in integrating into Western institutions, sought to develop alternative and competing regional institutions, and started to actively oppose leading Western institutions, such as the European Union (EU) and North Atlantic Treaty Organization (NATO).

In this report, we outline two categories of Russian views of the current international order: its fundamental logic and its components. Russian leaders and mainstream analysts see the current order's logic as U.S. domination and hegemony. They see expanding U.S. control achieved through regime change and disingenuous support for "liberal democracy." From a Russian perspective, the United States no longer has the power to back up this unilateral approach, and thus the current international order is not sustainable.

At the same time, Russia sees the potential for cooperation and collaboration in some components of the order, but not others. In particular, Russia supports the United Nations system because it bolsters Russia's position as a great power. Russia has also joined and actively participates in major international economic institutions, including the World Bank, the International Monetary Fund, and, more recently, the World Trade Organization. By contrast, where Russia sees elements of the U.S.-led order threatening its security or undermining its influence in its own neighborhood, it has pursued policies to undermine the current order. It has actively opposed the EU and NATO expanding into the former Soviet world and has increasingly sought to undermine these organizations. Russia supports alterna-

---

[1] Since the end of the Cold War, a series of pro-democracy and pro-Western protests have led to changes in government in the post-Soviet space; these have been referred to as *color revolutions* because participants often used flowers or colors as symbols. While Western governments have a positive view of these events as the expression of free choice by the citizenry, Russian analysts and officials describe the color revolutions as Western-organized coups, designed to subvert the legitimate authorities.

tive multilateral political and security agreements within its region—such as the Collective Security Treaty Organization and the Eurasian Economic Union—in part to compete with the EU and NATO. Russia has also bolstered ties with China through support for institutions that are outside of the U.S.-led order, including the Asian Infrastructure Investment Bank and a convention on information security. While arms control, in theory, has the potential to fit Russia's desires for the international order, Russia appears unlikely to agree to new confidence-building measures or arms control based on its increasing perception of a threat from the West.

Although there are a wide range of views within Russia, there is a fair degree of consensus among the government, major think tanks, and the Russian military. Some members of the opposition hold alternative beliefs that are more pro-Western, but their influence appears to be minimal. Analysts who are more radical and nationalist advocate a more aggressive approach to extending Russian influence. However, although the government and leading analysts have adopted nationalist rhetoric at times, it does not appear that radical thinkers have a significant influence over Russian policy.

This description of Russian views highlights the underlying choices for U.S. policy. Russian views of order are in clear opposition to the U.S. support for sustaining U.S. leadership and expanding democracy and Western institutions. Still, there are clear areas where cooperation with Russia is possible and areas where there is potential conflict. The desired U.S. approach to Russia with respect to order critically depends on how one evaluates two factors: (1) the importance of enabling former Soviet republics to freely join Western institutions and (2) whether Russia will limit its aggression in Europe if its interests are recognized. If one does not believe that Western institutions should necessarily be open to former Soviet countries, nor that Russia would undertake aggression if the West ceased to be active in the former Soviet countries, it would make sense to adapt the U.S. approach to order to recognize Russia's sphere of influence. However, if one believes that the former Soviet countries should be free to join Western institutions and that Russia has the potential to expand its influence and undertake aggression, it would make sense to "double down" the existing approach to order while bolstering U.S. support for its partners. Within the constraints of U.S. and European politics, probably neither a pure strategy of limiting enlargement or one of doubling down is feasible. U.S. policy toward the European political and security order will likely involve some elements of both.

Acknowledgments

We would like to thank the many individuals who took the time to speak with us about their opinions on this subject. Their candor and insight were invaluable. We also very much appreciate the input from the participants in an April 2016 workshop at the RAND Corporation on Russian views of order. Their contributions significantly advanced our understanding of this issue. The RAND team working on the Building a Sustainable International Order project—Michael Mazarr, Astrid Stuth Cevallos, and Miranda Priebe—also helped bring this paper to fruition. Jamie Greenberg and Allison Kerns offered editorial assistance. We would also like to thank Alina Polyakova, Thomas Wright, and Christopher Chivvis for their helpful suggestions. Finally, we express our appreciation to the Office of Net Assessment for sponsoring this work. Any errors are, of course, our own.

Abbreviations

ABM	anti-ballistic missile
BRICS	Brazil, Russia, India, China, and South Africa
CFE	Conventional Forces in Europe
CSCE	Commission on Security and Cooperation in Europe
CIS	Commonwealth of Independent States
CSTO	Collective Security Treaty Organization
EU	European Union
G-7	Group of Seven
G-8	Group of Eight
IMF	International Monetary Fund
INF	Intermediate-Range Nuclear Forces
ISIS	Islamic State of Iraq and Syria
NATO	North Atlantic Treaty Organization
OSCE	Organization for Security and Cooperation in Europe
START	Strategic Arms Reduction Treaty

UN	United Nations
USSR	Union of Soviet Socialist Republics
WTO	World Trade Organization

CHAPTER ONE

Introduction

Russian views about the current international order are of growing concern to the United States and its Western allies. In his speech at the Valdai International Discussion Club's annual meeting in 2014,[1] Russian President Vladimir Putin argued that the Western system of order threatened Russian interests, and he urged the development of a new world order that is more friendly to Russian interests.[2] A recent Russian documentary titled "World Order" reiterated these concerns and hinted that Russia and the North Atlantic Treaty Organization (NATO) were headed toward conflict because of incompatible views of the international order.[3] U.S. policymakers—including Ashton Carter, former Secretary of Defense under the Barack Obama administration—have argued that Russia offers a significant challenge to the international

---

[1] The Valdai International Discussion Club, established in 2004, is an organization that brings together Russian and international scholars and experts to discuss economic and political issues affecting Russian domestic and foreign affairs.

[2] Putin explained, "Instead of establishing a new balance of power, essential for maintaining order and stability, they took steps that threw the system into sharp and deep imbalance. The Cold War ended, but it did not end with the signing of a peace treaty with clear and transparent agreements on respecting existing rules or creating new rules and standards. This created the impression that the so-called 'victors' in the Cold War had decided to pressure events and reshape the world to suit their own needs and interests" (Vladimir Putin, "Meeting of the Valdai International Discussion Club," Sochi, Russia: Valdai International Discussion Club, October 24, 2014b).

[3] Ivan Krastev, "Why Putin Loves Trump," *New York Times*, January 12, 2016. To view the documentary, see Russian Federation, "Miroporyadok [World Order]," documentary, December 2015.

order through its annexation of Crimea and support for separatism in eastern Ukraine.[4]

This report examines Russian views of the current regional and international order and seeks to explain the origins of these views. By *international order*, we mean "the body of rules, norms, and institutions that govern relations among the key players in the international environment."[5] We analyze two kinds of views of the international order: (1) the order's fundamental logic, meaning how rules, institutions, and norms influence state behavior; and (2) the order's components, such as regional institutions; arms control agreements; international economic institutions; and norms of sovereignty, democracy, and human rights.[6] We find that Russia sees the overall logic of the current U.S.-led order as the embodiment of U.S. hegemony—and thus as threatening to Russia's interests and security. Nevertheless, Russian and U.S. interests align on some components of the order but diverge on others. Russia opposes the European Union (EU), NATO, and other institutions that it sees as threatening its security and influence within its "near abroad" (meaning Russia's perceived sphere of influence, which Russian analysts characterize as the former Soviet Union minus the Baltic states). At the same time, Russia participates and supports other elements of the order, such as the United Nations (UN) and arms control agreements.

To explain Russia's approach to order, we analyze the underlying interests guiding Russian foreign policy and examine Russian views of

---

[4] Robert Burns, "Carter Says Russia, China Potentially Threaten Global Order," *Military.com*, November 8, 2015.

[5] See Michael Mazarr, Miranda Priebe, Andrew Radin, and Astrid Stuth Cevallos, *Understanding the Current International Order*, Santa Monica, Calif.: RAND Corporation, RR-1598-OSD, 2016, p. 7.

[6] Mazarr et al., 2016, p. 7. A complete list of suborders includes the United Nations system; regional military alliances; regional political and economic organizations; international economic institutions; bilateral and multilateral arms control treaties; multilateral agreements to manage the global commons; norms of sovereignty, democracy, and human rights; and associated institutions.

its recent history. Drawing from existing work, we highlight the following five core interests that guide Russian foreign policy:

1. defense of the country and the regime
2. influence in the near abroad
3. a vision of Russia as a great power
4. noninterference in domestic affairs
5. political and economic cooperation as a partner equal to other great powers.

Russia's approach to order is also informed by its perceptions of the early post–Cold War period. Russian leaders contend that they attempted to pursue integration with the West following the Cold War and that this effort failed because the West would not recognize Russia's interests. This failure also leads current Russian leaders and analysts to question the wisdom of further close integration with the Western order.

Our goal in this report is not to explore Russian views of international order or international relations in the abstract. Rather, we are interested in Russian views of the current U.S.-led order because these views offer the most-direct implications for U.S. policy toward Russia. To this end, we focus primarily on official Russian government perspectives and mainstream foreign policy discourse, as these opinions likely will determine Russian foreign policy in the near future. We rely on English and Russian primary sources, including op-eds and leaders' speeches, memoirs, and other writings. We also use a range of secondary sources on Russian views, including think tank reports and academic work. Finally, we have conducted not-for-attribution discussions with a range of U.S. and Russian analysts and U.S. officials about Russian views.[7] We recognize that there is diversity of views within Russia, and after laying out the views of Russian leaders since the end of the Cold War, we highlight major alternative views within Russia.

---

[7] Of approximately 15 major interlocutors in our discussions, three were Russian analysts or former officials. Our discussions occurred between February and October 2016 and were undertaken in a variety of formats.

We also draw from other analysis on how Russia's activities relate to the international order,[8] recognizing that these works tend to analyze Russia's activities based on differing views of order rather than by scrutinizing Russia's views of order. In considering statements and analysis from Russian authors, especially from current political figures, we recognize that statements may be intended to achieve a particular political purpose or may not necessarily reflect those individuals' beliefs. Where we make claims that statements reflect beliefs or explain behavior, we attempt to identify a pattern of behavior that aligns with the observed statements. Further, where we state Russian views, we do not intend to offer either an endorsement or necessarily an assessment of their validity or factual correctness.

To analyze Russian views relative to those of the United States, it is useful to have a baseline for comparison. Recent RAND Corporation work has analyzed U.S. views of order in more detail, and we briefly summarize some early findings here. When U.S. analysts and policymakers describe the international order, they refer to the specific set of rules, institutions, and norms that emerged following World War II.[9] This order is often characterized as "liberal," reflecting increasingly shared principles of democratic governance and human rights, as well as the character of the trade and financial institutions that are part of the order. Although the demands and character of the current international order is contested within the U.S. policy discourse, there are certain agreed-upon principles in U.S. strategy documents, including "a rules-based free trade system, strong alliances and sufficient military capabilities for effective deterrence, multilateral cooperation/

---

[8]   See, for example, John J. Mearsheimer, "Why the Ukraine Crisis Is the West's Fault: The Liberal Delusions That Provoked Putin," *Foreign Affairs*, September/October 2014; Michael McFaul, Stephen Sestanovich, and John J. Mearsheimer, "Faulty Powers: Who Started the Ukraine Crisis?" *Foreign Affairs*, November/December 2014; and Paul Dibb, "Why Russia Is a Threat to the International Order," *The Strategist*, Australian Strategic Policy Institute, June 29, 2016.

[9]   This post–World War II order is composed of several reinforcing elements, including U.S. leadership; global institutions, such as the UN; interlocking global trade and financial institutions; international legal conventions, such as arms control regimes and laws of war; regional organizations; and developing norms. See Mazarr et al., 2016, p. 12.

international law to solve truly global problems . . . , and the spread of democracy."[10] Further, U.S. policy approaches often advocate continued U.S. leadership (hence the term *U.S.-led order*), countries' opportunity to join the Western-led order and develop democratic institutions, and the strengthening and enlarging of U.S.-backed alliances and regional organizations, including NATO and the EU.

Organization of This Report

The next chapter of this report analyzes the background of Russian foreign policy. We begin with this account for three reasons. First, there may be a tendency for Russian leaders or thinkers to use the term *order* loosely or strategically to justify or promote their foreign policy approach rather than to signify Russian views of the underlying rules, norms, and institutions of the current international environment. Outlining basic Russian foreign policy interests enables us to clearly identify Russia's thinking on these issues and situate Russia's views of order within its overall foreign policy. Second, and more critically, tracing Russia's underlying interests and understanding of history can explain Russian views of the components of order. Finally, understanding Russian views of history is important because Russian analysts and leaders routinely refer to the history of Russian foreign policy to explain their views of the current order.

Chapter Three is the heart of the analysis; it outlines Russia's current perspective on the international order and its policy and behavior toward various components of the order. Chapter Four explores alternative views within Russia. The final chapter concludes and offers policy implications.

---

[10] Mazarr et al., 2016, p. 45.

Background of Russian Foreign Policy

We posit that Russia's view of the international order stems from its overall approach to foreign policy. Therefore, by outlining some core Russian foreign policy interests and common views of its recent history, we can provide a foundation for Russia's views of the current international order and the background to explain the variation in Russia's approach to different components of the international order.

Key Interests Underlying Russian Foreign Policy After the Cold War

Drawing from existing work on Russian foreign policy and the statements of Russian leaders and analysts of Russia foreign policy, we identified five major interests that underlie Russian thinking, policy, and behavior since the end of the Cold War. We outlined these five major interests in Chapter One and describe them in detail below. These interests are neither all-encompassing of Russian views nor mutually exclusive. Rather, they highlight some key points of agreement that offer significant insight to explain Russian activity. These interests emphasize Russia's goal of preserving its own survival, prosperity, and dominance within its region while deepening engagement with the West at the same time.

1. Defense of the Country and Regime

Russian foreign policy is heavily influenced by perceptions of threat and vulnerability. These perceptions can include persistent concerns about external threat and domestic upheaval possibly supported by foreign parties.

Russia's geography—namely, its lack of major natural boundaries—and its history of foreign invasion have contributed to a national discourse of vulnerability and concern about foreign threat. Soviet leaders emphasized the threat posed by the forces of capitalism, and their efforts to exert control over the Warsaw Pact were partly motivated by the desire to have a buffer between the Soviet Union and the West.[1] Stephen Kotkin, a Princeton professor, observes, "Russia has felt perennially vulnerable and has often displayed a kind of defensive aggressiveness. . . . Today, too, smaller countries on Russia's borders are viewed less as potential friends than as potential beachheads for enemies."[2] Regardless of the real intentions of its neighbors, Russia takes seriously the possibility of invasion from abroad, which has sometimes manifested in its own aggressive behavior.

Russia's history, including the 1917 Communist revolution and the dissolution of the Soviet Union in 1991, has also led Russian leaders to be concerned about internal domestic upheaval. Gleb Pavlovsky, a former advisor to Putin, observes, "In the Kremlin establishment, ever since [then–Russian President Boris] Yeltsin's 1993 attack on the Parliament, there has been an absolute conviction that as soon as the power centre shifts, or if there is mass pressure, or the appearance of a popular leader, then everybody will be annihilated. It's a

---

[1] For example, in a 1946 message now known as the "Long Telegram," U.S. diplomat George Kennan noted, "At bottom of Kremlin's neurotic view of world affairs is traditional and instinctive Russian sense of insecurity. Originally, this was insecurity of a peaceful agricultural people trying to live on vast exposed plain in neighborhood of fierce nomadic peoples" (George Kennan, "The Charge in the Soviet Union (Kennan) to the Secretary of State," telegram to James F. Byrnes, Moscow, 1946).

[2] Stephen Kotkin, "Russia's Perpetual Geopolitics: Putin Returns to Historical Patterns," *Foreign Affairs*, May/June 2016; see also Jeffery Mankoff, *Russian Foreign Policy: The Return of Great Power Politics*, Lanham, Md.: Rowman & Littlefield Publishers, 2009, p. 3.

feeling of great vulnerability."[3] Because of the instability and lack of strong institutions within Russia, Russian leaders perhaps feel particular uncertainty about their personal position and safety. The fear of popular revolution is compounded by observations of U.S. support for the Arab Spring and "color revolutions," discussed in more detail in Chapter Three.[4]

Russian leaders' concerns about foreign and domestic threats are often linked. Russian leaders have often claimed that foreign enemies foment internal rebellion, and leaders have used this claim as a pretext to attack domestic opponents. During the Soviet period, for example, George Kennan, writing as "X" in 1947, noted that "internal opposition forces in Russia have consistently been portrayed as the agents of foreign forces of reaction," who in the case of the Soviet Union sought to overthrow the government.[5] Similarly, the Putin government has recently adopted legislation that enables the government to crack down on foreign organizations posing a "threat to the defense capability or security of the state, or public order, or to the health of population."[6] Whatever the real intentions of foreign organizations or the potential for foreign-led revolt, Russian leaders may fear these groups or may believe that they can attack such groups to strengthen the regime.

2. Influence in the Near Abroad

Russian leaders have consistently articulated a policy of maintaining close links with and influence within Russia's neighboring area. However, a major challenge in analyzing this objective is that the limits of Russia's interests are not well defined. Some sources highlight the use of the term *near abroad* to describe the region in which Russia seeks

---

[3]   Gleb Pavlovsky, "Putin's World Outlook," *New Left Review*, Vol. 88, July/August 2014, p. 62.

[4]   In short, since the end of the Cold War, a series of pro-democracy and pro-Western protests have led to changes in government in the post-Soviet space; these have been referred to as *color revolutions* because participants often used flowers or colors as symbols.

[5]   George Kennan (originally published as "X"), "The Sources of Soviet Conduct," *Foreign Affairs*, July 1947, pp. 569–570.

[6]   Priyanka Boghani, "New Russia Bill Targets 'Undesirable' Foreign Organizations," PBS Frontline, January 21, 2015.

the most-direct influence and control. But the near abroad does not have an uncontested geographic range. Russian analysts and accounts characterize the near abroad as countries that were formerly part of the Soviet Union, with the exception of the Baltics, noting that Russia no longer has significant influence or interests in the Baltic states.[7] At the same time, Russia is active in the Baltic states, especially through its engagement with the Russian minority. Further, Russia has degrees of influence beyond the former Soviet states to the rest of the former Communist world, especially with Slavic-speaking countries, such as Bulgaria and Serbia.[8] Hence, it may make the most sense to describe the geographic extent of Russia's desired influence as a set of concentric circles, with greater desired (though not necessarily achieved) interests in the more-central circles. In Figure 2.1, we offer one potential mapping of Russia's desired influence, with Russia, Belarus, Central Asia,

---

[7]   Russian analysts and U.S. analysts of Russia (in discussions conducted between February and October 2016) observe that Russia no longer thinks of the Baltics as within its direct sphere of influence, although it does retain elements of influence within the Baltics. Furthermore, Carnegie Moscow Center Director Dmitri V. Trenin observes,

> When in 2003 Russia redeployed forces from the Balkans and "conceded" the Baltics— under Putin, unlike in the Yeltsin period, there was no vociferous campaign protesting their membership, just clenched teeth—this regrouping was done to better consolidate Russia's few assets where it mattered most: in the CIS [Commonwealth of Independent States]. Moscow was ready to renounce its claim on a role in its old sphere of interest: Central and Southeastern Europe, and the Baltics. But it resolved not to allow further Western encroachments into the territory it felt was its "historical space." (Dmitri V. Trenin, *Post-Imperium: A Eurasian Story*, Washington, D.C.: Carnegie Endowment for International Peace, 2011, p. 107)

The absence of discussion of the Baltics within the 2013 Foreign Policy Concept, in contrast with the Caucuses, Ukraine, and Central Asia, is also striking (see Ministry of Foreign Affairs of the Russian Federation, *Concept of the Foreign Policy of the Russian Federation*, February 12, 2013). See Marlène Laruelle, *The "Russian World": Russia's Soft Power and Geopolitical Imagination*, Washington, D.C.: Center on Global Interests, May 2015, p. 1.

[8]   See, for example, Gatis Pelnens, ed., *The "Humanitarian Dimension" of Russian Foreign Policy Toward Georgia, Moldova, Ukraine, and the Baltic States*, Riga: Centre for East European Policy Studies, International Centre for Defence Studies, Centre for Geopolitical Studies, School for Policy Analysis at the National University of Kyiv-Mohyla Academy, Foreign Policy Association of Moldova, and International Centre for Geopolitical Studies, 2009, p. 18; and Heather Conley, James Mina, Ruslan Stefanov, and Martin Vladimirov, *The Kremlin Playbook: Understanding Russian Influence in Central and Eastern Europe*, Center for Strategic and International Studies, October 2016.

Figure 2.1
Russia's Desired Spheres of Influence

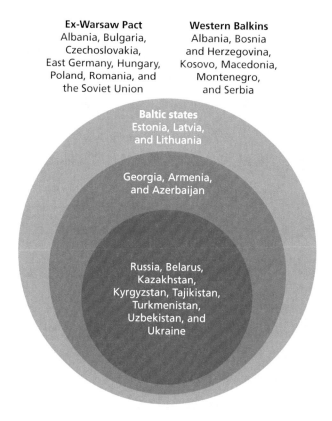

Ex-Warsaw Pact
Albania, Bulgaria,
Czechoslovakia,
East Germany, Hungary,
Poland, Romania, and
the Soviet Union

Western Balkins
Albania, Bosnia
and Herzegovina,
Kosovo, Macedonia,
Montenegro,
and Serbia

Baltic states
Estonia, Latvia,
and Lithuania

Georgia, Armenia,
and Azerbaijan

Russia, Belarus,
Kazakhstan,
Kyrgyzstan, Tajikistan,
Turkmenistan,
Uzbekistan, and
Ukraine

RAND *RR1826-2.1*

and Ukraine at the center and diminishing influence in the Caucuses,
the Baltic states, and then the Western Balkans (such as Bosnia and
Herzegovina, Kosovo, and Serbia) and countries of the former Warsaw
Pact (such as Bulgaria, Hungary, Poland, and Romania).[9]

---

[9]   Russia's interests and policy in each of these countries may be contested, and there may
be different ways to draw this diagram accordingly. This breakdown draws on the sources
cited in this document and our discussions with various analysts. See also, Trenin, 2011,
Chapter 2.

Russia's belief that it is a great power (as discussed later) and its concern about maintaining a buffer from foreign invasion may inform its interest in its neighborhood, but this desire for regional influence most likely runs even deeper than strategic concerns alone would suggest.[10] Russian and Western analysts cite a longstanding "imperial" identity, drawing from Russia's imperial expansion in the 16th through 19th centuries and the record of the Soviet Union.[11] Igor Zevelev, former director of the MacArthur Foundation's Russia office, writes that Russian identity includes the "'Little Russians' (Ukrainians), the 'White Russians' (Byelorussians), and the 'Great Russians' (ethnic Russians)."[12] Russian identity is also connected with the other post-Soviet states, including Central Asia, given their shared Soviet past and use of the Russian language. Russia's link, responsibility, and leadership over its region are currently articulated as part of Russian policy through the term *Russkiy Mir*, or Russian world, meaning support for Russia's "compatriots."[13] Still, there is a great diversity of the countries and populations that might fall under the Russkiy Mir, and there is no single definition of what defines or limits Russia's desired links with countries or individuals. Potential shared attributes may include, among other elements, the ethnic Russian population, Russian-language speakers, adherents of the Russian Orthodox Church, citizens of the former

---

[10] Olga Oliker and colleagues write, "Why is it so important to Russia to maintain influence [in its near abroad]? The reasons stem from Russia's quest for prestige, its history, its economic priorities, and its fundamental security concerns" (Olga Oliker, Keith Crane, Lowell H. Schwartz, and Catherine Yusupov, *Russian Foreign Policy: Sources and Implications*, RAND Corporation, Santa Monica, Calif.: RAND Corporation, MG-768-AF, 2009, p. 93).

[11] Trenin describes Russia as "post-imperium," noting the Russian and Soviet history of imperial control and the loss of the empire in the 1990s (Trenin, 2011, introduction). Ronald Suny writes, "From its beginning, then, Russian identity was bound up with the supranational world of belief, the political world loosely defined by the ruling dynasty, and was contrasted to 'others' at the periphery" (Ronald Grigor Suny, *The Empire Strikes Out: Imperial Russia, "National" Identity, and Theories of Empire*, Chicago: University of Chicago Press, 1997, p. 20).

[12] Igor Zevelev, *NATO's Enlargement and Russian Perceptions of Eurasian Political Frontiers*, Garmisch-Partenkirchen, Germany: George Marshall European Center for Security Studies, undated, p. 17.

[13] See Laruelle, 2015, pp. 4, 19.

Soviet Union and their dependents, and Slavic-language speakers.[14] The reach of the concept of the Russkiy Mir may thus be quite broad, and the identification of shared links and connections may be politicized and adapted based on other Russian foreign policy goals.[15]

Analysts emphasize the continuing influence of these supranationalist views of Russian identity, especially the view that countries emerging from the former Soviet republics are not truly independent countries.[16] Trenin observes, "For many in Russia, the new states are not yet quite states. Interestingly, Moscow's political relations with them are still managed by the Kremlin chief of staff, rather than the foreign minister. For many in the new states, the CIS is a holdover from the imperial era, a club in which they are less equal than the former hegemon."[17] Indeed, a long-running survey of Russian elites shows a changing, but generally commonly held, view that "the national interests of Russia for the most part extend beyond its existing territory," as shown in Figure 2.2. In 2012, there was a drop in respondents who viewed Russia's interests beyond the country, perhaps corresponding to domestic protests in Russia in 2011 and 2012.

There is also a question of how to characterize the type of influence Russia has or pursues. Although the answer may vary by case, analysts have offered at least three ways to frame this influence:

1. Countries do not make any important foreign and security policy decisions without consulting Russia.
2. Russia requires that when it "picks up the phone," leaders follow through on Russia's requests.

---

[14] Laruelle writes, "As was the case with the Russian World, the concept of the 'compatriot' was intended to remain fuzzy. As early as 2001, Putin insisted on its fluidity: 'The compatriot is not only a legal category. More importantly, it is not an issue of status or favoritism. It is primarily a matter of personal choice. Of selfidentification. I would even say, of spiritual self-identification'" (Laruelle, 2015, p. 8).

[15] We are grateful to Alina Polyakova for this observation.

[16] Author discussions with U.S. and Russian analysts, Cambridge, UK, and Washington, D.C., February–April 2016.

[17] Trenin, 2011, p. 80.

Figure 2.2
Survey Results on the Scope of Russia's National Interests

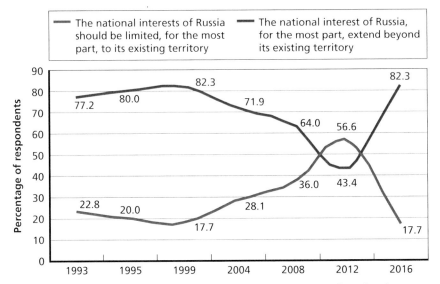

SOURCE: Sharon Werning Rivera, James Bryan, Brisa Camacho-Lovell, Carlos Fineman, Nora Klemmer, and Emma Raynor, *2016 Hamilton College Levitt Poll: The Russian Elite 2016—Perspectives on Foreign Policy and Domestic Policy*, Clinton, N.Y.: Hamilton College, Arthur Levitt Public Affairs Center, May 11, 2016, p. 15. Used with permission.
NOTE: Question wording: "There are various opinions about the national interests of Russia. Which of the two assertions below are closer to your point of view?
  1. The national interests of Russia should be limited, for the most part, to its existing territory.
  2. The national interests of Russia, for the most part, extend beyond its existing territory."
Responses of "don't know" were excluded from the analysis.
RAND *RR1826-2.2*

3. Russian-backed organizations, including the Collective Security Treaty Organization (CSTO), CIS, and Russian nongovernmental organizations, have links and ties with the country in question.[18]

---

[18] Author discussions with U.S. and Russian think tank analysts, Washington, D.C., April–May 2016. See also Pelnens, 2009.

3. A Vision of Russia as a Great Power

Russia has consistently described itself as a great power.[19] At a minimum, this vision includes Russia's desire to participate in deciding global issues and to have a sphere of influence in its region.

In addition to consistently referring to Russia as a great power, Russian officials have advocated a "multipolar" vision of the world, apparently indicating that they think Russia is and should remain one of several major powers.[20] Even given Russia's significant financial problems in 1992, Yeltsin responded negatively to an offer of "assistance" from U.S. President Bill Clinton, noting, "We're not asking for handouts. Russia is a great power."[21] In 2008, then–Russian President Dmitry Medvedev included multipolarity as one of five key principles of Russian foreign policy, saying, "The world should be multipolar. Unipolarity is unacceptable; domination is impermissible. We cannot accept a world order in which all decisions are taken by one country, even such a serious and authoritative country as the United States of America."[22] This principle is stated in several official documents. For example, the Russian National Security Strategy of 2009 stated Russia's intention to actively participate "in the development of the multipolar model of the international system," while the 2013 Foreign Policy Concept identified the goal of "securing [Russia's] high standing in

---

[19] Hill and Gaddy note that Putin highlighted "*derzhavnost*'—the belief that Russia is destined always to be a great power (*derzhava*) exerting its influence abroad" as one of the values within the "Russian idea" in his 1999 "Millennium Message" (Fiona Hill and Clifford Gaddy, *Mr. Putin: Operative in the Kremlin*, Washington, D.C.: Brookings Institution Press, 2013, pp. 38–39, 238). Further, Mankoff identifies the great-power identity as a dominant feature of Russia's foreign policy since 1990 (Mankoff, 2009, p. 12).

[20] Russian analysts' discussion of multipolarity and unipolarity may, to some degree, conflate their view of the current balance of power with how decisions are carried out (i.e., unilateralism or multilateralism). We keep the Russian use of these terms in this report.

[21] Strobe Talbott, *The Russia Hand: A Memoir of Presidential Diplomacy*, New York: Random House, 2002.

[22] Paul Reynolds, "New Russian World Order: The Five Principles," BBC News, 2008. Olga Oliker and colleagues write that during Putin's term from 2004 to 2008, a consensus emerged that Russia's foreign policy goals were to "solidify its increasing economic success and strive to be perceived as a 'modern great power' or a 'normal great power'" (Oliker et al., 2009, p. 87).

the international community as one of the influential and competitive poles of the modern world."[23]

Russian analysts similarly note Russia's contention that it is a great power. For instance, Trenin writes that Russia "refuses to accept the rank of a middle power with merely a regional role. It sees itself as a global actor, playing in the big leagues."[24] More recently, Fyodor Lukyanov—editor of *Russia in Global Affairs* and research director for the Valdai International Discussion Club—writes that Russia cannot be treated as just another country, as the United States and European states apparently intend:

> For all practical intents and purposes, a large country with the mentality and history of an independent great power simply could not overnight turn itself into a "big Poland" and follow in the footsteps of states seeking admission to the EU and NATO— institutions that, in any event, never offered membership to Russia.[25]

These accounts imply that Russia should not be treated as just any other member of an international institution, but rather as a higher-status member with rights equal to other great powers, including the United States.[26]

---

[23] Russian Federation, *National Security Strategy of the Russian Federation to 2020*, May 12, 2009; Ministry of Foreign Affairs of the Russian Federation, 2013.

[24] Trenin, 2011, p. 210. He further observes, "in the later thinking of the Kremlin, the global anarchy prevailing after the end of the bipolar era can best be structured as a global oligarchy, also known as multipolarity. This is not an analytical conclusion, but an active posture" (p. 210). Carnegie senior associate Lilia Shevtsova also highlights the importance of the idea of *derzhavnichestvo*—that "Russia is a great power or it is nothing" (Lilia Shevtsova, *Russia: Lost in Transition*, Washington, D.C.: Carnegie Endowment for International Peace, 2007, p. 3).

[25] Fyodor Lukyanov, "The Lost Twenty-Five Years," *Russia in Global Affairs*, February 28, 2016a.

[26] Yeltsin similarly emphasized that Russia sought a position as an equal partner of the United States, saying, "Russia isn't Haiti, and we won't be treated as though we were. That won't be sustainable and it won't be acceptable. Just forget it! What we insist on is equality.

Russia's great-power status, from its perspective, implies particular rights within its immediate region, a special role in deciding international disputes, cooperation with other great powers, and a greater degree of autonomy or sovereignty. Medvedev justified Russia's sphere of influence based on its great-power status, arguing, "Russia, just like other countries in the world, has regions where it has its privileged interests. In these regions, there are countries with which we have traditionally had friendly cordial relations, historically special relations."[27] Russia also seeks to be a leading participant in resolving ongoing international conflicts. American diplomat Richard Holbrooke writes that during the negotiations in Bosnia in the 1990s, "we felt that Moscow's primary goal was neither to run nor to wreck the negotiations. Rather, what it wanted most was to restore a sense, however symbolic, that [Russia] still mattered in the world."[28] In the ongoing Syrian civil war, Russia has helped negotiate the disarmament of Syria's chemical weapons, reinforced its military presence, conducted extensive air strikes in support of the Bashar al-Assad regime, and participated in negotiations ostensibly in support of a ceasefire.[29] In Ukraine, Russia has

---

What I began with Bush and have developed with Clinton—an equal partnership—is in the interest of both our people" (Talbott, 2002, p. 197).

[27] Reynolds, 2008. Russian-born international relations professor Andrei Tsygankov also writes, "Post–cold war Russia seeks to act globally mainly to secure its status as a regional great power" (Andrei P. Tsygankov, "Preserving Influence in a Changing World," *Problems of Post-Communism*, Vol. 58, No. 2, 2011, p. 41).

[28] Richard Holbrooke, *To End a War: The Conflict in Yugoslavia—America's Inside Story—Negotiating with Milosevic*, New York: Modern Library, 1999, p. 117. Along these lines, in both Bosnia and Kosovo, Russia refused to have its peacekeeping forces under a NATO command structure. Instead, Russia was willing to deploy forces only under a U.S. commander who was also dual-hatted as a NATO commander. See Talbott, 2002; and Holbrooke, 1999, pp. 214, 259.

[29] Prominent Russian commentator Dmitri Kiselyov observed about the proposed peace agreement, "The essence is that two great powers, the United States and Russia, are taking direct responsibility for peace in Syria" (Howard Amos, "Russia Welcomes Syria Ceasefire as Proof of Great Power Status," *International Business Times*, February 29, 2016). Still, as discussed later, some U.S. officials and analysts are critical of Russia's actions, especially the bombing of civilian targets, and skeptical of Russia's intent to achieve a ceasefire (see Amos,

preferred that negotiations take place under the Normandy Format, including France, Germany, Russia, and Ukraine, which may be desirable, in part, because it signifies Russia's status as a leading great power in Europe and excludes the United States.[30]

Russia has also sought to strengthen its position as a great power through its support for the UN; Brazil, Russia, India, China, and South Africa (BRICS) association; and other forums discussed later that emphasize the role and authority of regional great powers.[31] Russia's cooperation with China is also significant, as both countries seek a greater say in the world as great powers. For example, both have conducted joint naval exercises in such areas as the South China Sea, have worked together through the Shanghai Cooperation Organisation to limit U.S. military presence in Central Asia, and are pursuing an international convention on information security.[32]

Russia's view of its great-power status also may be connected with a concept of its own desired autonomy and sovereignty. Some analysts write that Russia seeks full or absolute sovereignty or autonomy and sees itself in a small category of great powers that have such sovereignty, including China and the United States. Other countries, including the European powers, are less sovereign, especially because they need to consult with the United States or other countries to develop or execute their policy. Russia may seek and be able to continue its greater auton-

---

2016; Michelle Nichols and Yara Bayoumy, "U.S. Slams Russian 'Barbarism' in Syria," Reuters, September 25, 2016; "Syria Crisis: Putin 'Confident' on Chemical Weapons Plan," BBC News, September 19, 2013; and "Syria Conflict: US-Russia Brokered Truce to Start at Weekend," BBC News, February 22, 2016).

[30] One Russian analyst lauded the Normandy Format as "the best possible format": "When evaluating the efficiency of the 'Normandy Four,' one should remember that the Ukrainian conflict is less a clash for Ukraine, its national political regime and foreign policy orientation but more for the rules of the international order and relations between great powers in particular" (Dmitry Suslov, "'Normandy Four': The Best Possible Format," Valdai International Discussion Club, February 10, 2015).

[31] See Alexander Lukin, "Russia in a Post-Bipolar World," *Survival: Global Politics and Strategy*, Vol. 58, No. 1, February–March 2016, pp. 104–107.

[32] "Declaration of Heads of Member States of SCO," Astana, Kazakhstan, *China Daily*, July 5, 2005.

omy by avoiding alliances or binding agreements with other powers, as well as by maintaining economic strength and military power.[33]

4. Noninterference in Domestic Affairs

Russian leaders often insist that noninterference is a key principle of global governance and international affairs. Russian officials in particular emphasize that the right of noninterference should not be violated without approval of the UN Security Council.[34]

Indeed, in our description in the next section of Russian views on the current order, we highlight growing concern within Russia about an upward trend of Western interference. Much of Russia's emphasis on noninterference no doubt stems from its desire to protect the regime and its interests in its near abroad. This points to a fundamental irony—namely, that while declaring the importance of noninterference, it seeks to maintain influence in the affairs of its neighbors. Indeed, from Russia's point of view, its prerogative of a great power permits it an exception from the principle of noninterference and the exclusive ability to interfere in the affairs of its neighbors.[35]

In the unique immediate post–Cold War period, Russia recognized that human rights are not exclusively the responsibility of the internal affairs of states.[36] Nevertheless, since then, Russia has increas-

---

[33] Hill and Gaddy, 2013, pp. 317–319; and Angela Stent, *The Limits of Partnership: U.S.-Russian Relations in the Twenty-First Century*, Princeton, N.J.: Princeton University Press, 2014, p. 258.

[34] Before returning to the presidency in 2012, Putin noted the importance of the "United Nations and its Security Council to effectively counter the dictates of some countries and their arbitrary actions in the world arena," adding, "Nobody has the right to usurp the prerogatives and powers of the U.N., particularly the use of force against sovereign nations" (Vladimir Putin, "Russia and the Changing World," RT News, February 27, 2012).

[35] Author discussions with U.S. analysts, Washington, D.C., April 2016.

[36] In the 1991 Moscow meeting of the Conference on the Human Dimension of the Commission on Security and Cooperation in Europe (CSCE), Russia signed on to the concluding document:

> The participating States emphasize that issues relating to human rights, fundamental freedoms, democracy and the rule of law are of international concern, as respect for these rights and freedoms constitutes one of the foundations of the international order. *They categorically and irrevocably declare that the commitments undertaken in the field of the*

ingly emphasized noninterference as a recurring theme in its foreign policy discourse. In the late 1990s, noninterference was frequently raised in the context of the military conflict in Chechnya, where Russia faced significant criticism for human rights violations. Following the Organization for Security and Cooperation in Europe (OSCE) Summit in Turkey in 1999, for example, Russian leaders emphasized that Western European countries had "no right to criticize Russia for Chechnya," and that "We will, in the most decided way, deflect all attempts at interference in Russia's internal affairs, no matter under which pretext."[37] Russian officials have also cited the noninterference principle while opposing Western intervention. In the case of Kosovo, for example, former U.S. Deputy Secretary of State Strobe Talbott writes, "Russian politicians, generals, and commentators speculated with mounting alarm that the air campaign the U.S. and its allies were getting ready to unleash against Serbia was a warm-up for a future war with Russia that might begin with the West's claim that it was defending the rights of the Chechens."[38] Russian officials and analysts have criticized the West for inconsistency in its approach to noninterference, noting U.S. support for Western-backed secession movements in East Timor and Kosovo but opposition to Russian activities in South Ossetia and Crimea.[39]

Russian leaders have stated that the principle of noninterference applies to the near abroad. Then–Russian President Mikhail Gorbachev's resignation speech, for example, noted that Russia had "renounced intervention in other people's affairs and the use of troops

---

human dimension of the CSCE are matters of direct and legitimate concern to all participating States and do not belong exclusively to the internal affairs of the State concerned. (CSCE, *The Human Dimension*, Washington, D.C., 1991, emphasis in original)

[37] "Yeltsin: West Has 'No Right' to Criticize Chechen Campaign," CNN, November 18, 1999; and Mark Tran, "Russia Will Pursue Chechnya Campaign Says Yeltsin," *The Guardian*, November 15, 1999.

[38] Talbott, 2002, p. 301.

[39] Nadezhda K. Arbatova and Alexander A. Dynkin, "World Order After Ukraine," *Survival: Global Politics and Strategy*, Vol. 58, No. 1, February–March 2016, p. 85.

beyond the borders of our country."[40] The charter of the CIS included principles of "respect for sovereignty of member states, for imprescriptible right of people for self-determination and the right to dispose their destiny without interference from outside."[41] Nevertheless, analysts of Russian activity emphasize that Russia's actual practice instead tends toward exerting informal influence over its neighbors.[42]

5. Political and Economic Cooperation as a Partner Equal to Other Great Powers

Since the end of the Cold War, Russia has frequently sought greater partnership and cooperation with the West. However, in accordance with its vision of itself as a great power, Russia seeks cooperation not just as another country but as an "equal" partner. It is sometimes vague which countries or entities Russia sees itself as equal to—the United States, the leading European powers, or such organizations as the EU or NATO—but at a minimum, Russia seeks outsized recognition, status, and authority in any cooperative relationship.

The initial post–Cold War period began a new era of close cooperation between Russia and the United States. Strobe Talbott writes that Gorbachev and his staff "came up with a new word to describe the ties they wanted to have with the U.S.: partnership. . . . As partners, the U.S. and the Soviet Union could move beyond 'negative peace'— the avoidance of war—toward joint management of the world's problems."[43] Yeltsin continued to pursue partnership with the West, referring frequently to the term, while developing a personal relationship with President Clinton.[44] The 1993 Russian Foreign Policy Concept envisioned that "Russia will strive toward the stable development

---

[40] Zbigniew Brzezinski and Paige Sullivan, eds., *Russia and the Commonwealth of Independent States: Documents, Data, and Analysis*, Armonk, N.Y.: M.E. Sharpe, 1997, p. 49.

[41] "Commonwealth of Independent States: Charter," *International Legal Materials*, Vol. 34, No. 5, September 1995.

[42] Author discussions with U.S. analysts, Washington, D.C., March 2016.

[43] Talbott, 2002, p. 19.

[44] Talbott, 2002, pp. 163, 183, 197.

of relations with the United States, with a view toward strategic partnership and, in the future, toward alliance."[45]

Although, to some extent, Vladimir Putin repudiated Yeltsin's policies as weak, he also pursued a closer relationship with the West in areas of mutual interest. Putin pursued closer ties with the EU and—following September 11, 2001—was supportive of the U.S. war on terror. Russian professors Nadezhda Arbatova and Alexander Dynkin highlight Putin's cooperative efforts in the early 2000s, noting "The Kremlin offered the U.S. its unprecedented support as a true ally in setting up an antiterrorist coalition," and "Putin reiterated that Russia would reconsider its position if it were to be included in this process."[46]

From 2008 to 2012, the Medvedev government emphasized closer relations with the West, apparently with the support of Putin, who had become the Prime Minister. Medvedev included "no isolation" as one of his five principles, noting, "We will develop, as far as possible, friendly relations both with Europe and with the United States of America, as well as with other countries of the world."[47] In 2010, the foreign minister, Sergey Lavrov, emphasized the "teamwork philosophy" underlying Russian foreign policy, explaining that improved connections with Russia's neighbors could enable modernization and economic development.[48] However, Medvedev and other Russian leaders saw Russia as the leader of a major bloc, not just another country: "The end of the Cold War made it possible to establish genuinely equal cooperation between Russia, the European Union, and North America as three branches of European civilization."[49]

---

[45] Ministry of Foreign Affairs of the Russian Federation, *Conception of the Foreign Policy of the Russian Federation*, 1993.

[46] Arbatova and Dynkin, 2016, p. 83.

[47] Reynolds, 2008.

[48] Sergey Lavrov, "The Euro-Atlantic Region: Equal Security for All," *Russia in Global Affairs*, July 7, 2010.

[49] Igor Zevelev, "The Russian World Boundaries: Russia's National Identity Transformation and New Foreign Policy Doctrine," *Russia in Global Affairs*, June 7, 2014.

While the Ukraine crisis might indicate a shift away from a desire for close cooperation with the West, Russian leaders continue to emphasize their desire for cooperation on what they describe as equal terms. In a March 2016 essay, Lavrov explains, "we are not seeking confrontation with the United States, or the European Union, or NATO. On the contrary, Russia is open to the widest possible cooperation with its Western partners." Lavrov clarifies that cooperation would be on Russian terms of a "universal feeling of equality and equally guaranteed security."[50]

Evolution of Russia's Views of the U.S.-Led Order

In addition to the principles outlined in the previous section, Russia's current view of the U.S.-led order is significantly informed by its view of the post–Cold War period. In particular, Russian leaders and analysts contend that Russia sought close cooperation with the West in the early 1990s and that this cooperation went poorly for Russia. Most critically, when Russia sought integration into Western institutions, the West did not adapt the major institutions—including NATO, the EU, and the World Trade Organization (WTO)—to incorporate Russia and respect Russian interests. The record of these events contributes to the Russian view that it would not be feasible for Russia to attempt to join the EU or NATO in the future and that it is necessary for Russia to develop alternative institutions. Russian officials and analysts also began to view the U.S.-led order as threatening, rather than simply misguided, following U.S. military interventions undertaken without UN approval and growing perceptions of the encroachment of the EU and NATO into Russia's sphere of influence. To inform the narrative of Russia's changing views of the U.S.-led order, we preview here some observations from our account of different components of order (see Chapter Three for further details).

---

[50] Lavrov, 2010.

Immediately following the Cold War, there was a brief period in which pro-Western officials under Yeltsin sought not only to integrate Russia into the West but also to model Russia on Western institutions. From around 1992 to 1993, for example, acting Prime Minister Yegor Gaidar pursued a policy of rapid liberalization and economic "shock therapy" recommended by Western officials, while Foreign Minister Andrei Kozyrev adopted a "romantic embrace" of the West.[51] Russia's foreign policy during this period was partly connected to a view proposed by Gorbachev that, as Lukyanov explains, "a new world order would emerge through the integration of East and West on a completely equal basis."[52] The belief that Russia would play a shared role in a new world order appears to have been encouraged by U.S. policymakers. For example, U.S. scholar Joshua Itzkowitz Shifrinson writes, "Baldly stated, the United States floated a cooperative grand design for postwar Europe in discussions with the Soviet Union in 1990, while creating a system dominated by the United States."[53] Russian analysts and officials' perception that there was a divergence between U.S. promises early in the post–Cold War period and U.S. policy thereafter soured Russian views of the future desirability to adapt Russia to integrate with Western institutions.

---

[51] Roland Dannreuther, *Russian Perceptions of the Atlantic Alliance*, Edinburgh, Scotland: Edinburgh University, 1997, p. 10. In December 1991, for example, Kozyrev stated that Russia viewed NATO "as one of the mechanisms for stability in Europe and in the world as a whole" (Dannreuther, 1997, p. 10) and even asked former U.S. President Richard Nixon to help him define Russia's national interests (see Andrew Kuchins and Igor Zevelev, "Russian Foreign Policy: Continuity in Change," *Washington Quarterly*, Vol. 35, No. 1, Winter 2012, pp. 148–149, 153; and Mankoff, 2009, p. 37).

[52] Lukyanov, 2016a; Fyodor Lukyanov, "Putin's Foreign Policy," *Foreign Affairs*, May/June 2016b, p. 32. Dannreuther similarly emphasizes that Gorbachev sought "a more cooperative and less conflictual East-West relationship which would provide the international framework for supporting his domestic economic reforms of *perestroika*," and highlights Gorbachev's embrace of concepts of "the Common European House (*Evropa, nash obshchii dom*)," "New Thinking (*novoe myshlenie*)," and "Freedom of Choice (*svoboda vybora*) for the countries of central and south-eastern Europe" (Dannreuther, 1997, p. 6).

[53] Joshua Itzkowitz Shifrinson, "Deal or No Deal? The End of the Cold War and the U.S. Offer to Limit NATO Expansion," *International Security*, Vol. 40, No. 4, Spring 2016, pp. 11–12.

By 1993, the policies championed by pro-Western officials, especially the domestic economic policies, were seen as a failure in Russia.[54] Gaidar was forced from office in 1992, and in 1996, Kozyrev was replaced by Yevgeny Primakov, who analysts describe as promoting a "straightforward realist conception of international affairs" promoting Russia as a great power.[55] While Russian leaders no longer sought to adopt the Western democratic models within Russia, they still sought membership, or at least a Russian voice, in the major Western institutions. For example, Yeltsin supported the potential candidacy of Russia in NATO and improved formal measures of consultation with NATO through the NATO-Russia Permanent Joint Council established by the NATO Russia Founding Act (discussed later). At the same time, Russian officials opposed what they saw as U.S. unilateralism, including NATO enlargement and intervention in Kosovo—manifested, for example, through Russia's attempted seizure of the Prishtina International Airport in 1999.[56] Russian frustration with the West also grew as a result of the perceived failure of Western assistance in the economic realm—for example, following the 1998 financial crisis. Still, throughout his presidency, Yeltsin did not abandon the principle of closer partnership and integration with the West, despite growing frustration with U.S. behavior. Upon taking over power from Yeltsin, Putin drew on the perception that Yeltsin's policies, especially those toward the West, had undermined Russia's position in the world. In his 1999 Millennium Message, for example, Putin explained that "Russia has [just] experienced one of the most difficult periods in its many centuries of history. Perhaps for the first time in 200–300 years, she faces the real danger of becoming not just a second but even a third tier country."[57] These perceptions appear to reflect widely growing frustration among

---

[54] Kuchins and Zevelev, for example, write, "The defeat of the liberal reformers, caused principally by the economic crisis in the early 1990s, shifted Russian foreign policy to more traditional realist concepts asserting national interests and expanding power and influence" (Kuchins and Zevelev, 2012, p. 153).

[55] Kuchins and Zevelev, 2012, p. 150; Mankoff, 2009, pp. 36, 38–39.

[56] Hill and Gaddy, 2013, pp. 299–300.

[57] Hill and Gaddy, 2013, p. 81.

many Russian elites of Russia's weakening position in the world, as well as a suspicion that closer relations with the West were not necessarily to Russia's benefit.[58]

Despite Putin's eventual harsh rhetoric toward the West, in the early period of his first term as President, he continued to pursue cooperation and integration with the West, including through closer relations with NATO and the EU.[59] For example, in March 2000, Putin was positive about the potential for Russia to join NATO if its interests were recognized and if it would be an equal (great-power) partner.[60] In a 2001 speech to the Bundestag (Germany's national parliament), Putin similarly emphasized that "the spirit of [democracy and freedom] filled the overwhelming majority of Russian citizens," and he urged cooperation and integration between Europe and Russia.[61] In 2004, Russia expressed only a mild negative response to the Baltic countries' accession to NATO.[62] Putin also launched Russia's effort to join the WTO. At the same time, Russia's policy was not as positive toward the West as under Yeltsin. For example, Lukyanov notes, "From the Russian point of view, a critical turning point came when NATO intervened in the Kosovo war in 1999. Many Russians—even strong advocates of liberal

---

[58] Hill and Gaddy write, "Soviet President Mikhail Gorbachev summed up the general elite consensus in Moscow. The West had taken advantage of Russia's weakness. The West's policy in Europe, the Balkans, and within the former Soviet Union, he asserted, 'is marked by a clear disrespect for Russia'" (Hill and Gaddy, 2013, p. 36).

[59] By one account, "for a brief period Putin pursued his own version of a 'reset' in U.S.-Russia relations" (Kuchins and Zevelev, 2012, p. 155; see also Mankoff, 2009, p. 31).

[60] In 2000, Putin answered a question about the potential membership of Russia in NATO by responding, "Why not? Why not? . . . I do not rule out such a possibility . . . in the case that Russia's interests will be reckoned with, if it will be an equal partner" (David Hoffman, "Putin on Joining NATO: 'If as Equals, Why Not?'" *Moscow Times*, March 7, 2000).

[61] See Vladimir Putin, "Speech in the Bundestag of the Federal Republic of Germany," Berlin: President of Russia, September 25, 2001.

[62] For example, in his 2005 address to the Federal Assembly, Putin only noted, "We hope that the new members of NATO and the European Union in the post-Soviet area will show their respect for human rights, including the rights of ethnic [Russian] minorities, through their actions" (Vladimir Putin, "Annual Address to the Federal Assembly of the Russian Federation," Moscow, April 25, 2005; see also Mankoff, 2009, p. 160).

reform—were appalled by NATO's bombing raids against Serbia, a European country with close ties to Moscow."[63]

Several factors in the mid-2000s contributed to growing skepticism that Russian interests as outlined earlier in this chapter could be achieved through integration into Western institutions. As described in detail in Chapter Three, Russia was disappointed in its ability to influence NATO decisionmaking,[64] was surprised at the resistance to its bid for WTO accession, and felt disrespect at the lack of special treatment from the EU.[65] Further, several U.S. policies in the early 2000s were perceived as threatening Russia's security and interests in its near abroad, including the color revolutions in Georgia in 2003 and Ukraine in 2004, U.S. plans for antiballistic missile defenses, and the invasion of Iraq without a UN mandate.[66] Russia's increasing wealth from oil and gas exports, which in early 2006 enabled it to pay off Western loans from the 1990s, likely also played a factor in changing Russian views.[67]

Trenin, writing in 2006, summarized the changing Russian view: "Until recently, Russia saw itself as Pluto in the Western solar system, very far from the center but still fundamentally a part of it. Now it has left that orbit entirely: Russia's leaders have given up on becoming part of the West and have started creating their own Moscow-centered system."[68] Although there were elements and periods of greater cooperation with the United States, after 2007, Russian relations with the United States began a clear downward trajectory, with Russia expressing increasing concern and bolstering alternative institutions. In Putin's 2007 speech at the Munich Conference on Security Policy, he heavily criticized the U.S.-led order by observing that the "unipolar model . . .

---

[63] Lukyanov, 2016b, p. 33.

[64] Dmitri Trenin, "Russia Leaves the West," *Foreign Affairs*, July/August 2006.

[65] Author discussion with U.S. and Russian analysts, Cambridge, UK, and Washington, D.C., February–April, 2016.

[66] As Hill and Gaddy explain, Putin "now saw the United States as irresponsible and incompetent—not just unchecked in its exercise in power" (Hill and Gaddy, 2013, p. 316).

[67] Kuchins and Zevelev, 2012, p. 155.

[68] Trenin, 2006.

has nothing in common with democracy" and "is not only unacceptable but also impossible,"[69] beginning a line of rhetoric and an increasingly negative view of the U.S.-led order that would continue through to the present.

From the perspective of Putin and other senior Russian officials, several events following 2007 reinforced the interpretation that the West's activities were, perhaps unintentionally, undermining Russian security; by 2012 or 2013, these events led to a growing view that the United States and the West were actively and intentionally threatening to Russia. For example, NATO's openness to having Ukraine and Georgia become members likely contributed to Russia's decision to undertake military action in Georgia. In addition, American support for the Arab Spring and military action against Libya, as discussed later, contributed to a perception that the United States and the West could and would undertake violent regime change. Putin appears to have drawn a clear line between the Arab Spring and Western support for democracy to the 2011–2012 protests in Russia against his reelection to the presidency.[70] Thus, from Putin's perspective, U.S. support for the pro-Western Maidan protestors in Ukraine (see Chapter Three), a country of major importance for Russia, led to a clear sign that the West was violating Russia's security and prerogatives as a great power. Still, despite growing suspicion of the United States and the West, Russian officials insisted on their desire for continued cooperation with the West where possible.[71]

---

[69] See Vladimir Putin, "Putin's Prepared Remarks at 43rd Munich Conference on Security Policy," Munich, February 12, 2007.

[70] In addition to further discussion about these events later in this report, see Hill and Gaddy, 2013, pp. 235, 305–311.

[71] In Putin's March 2014 speech, he explained,

> Like a mirror, the situation in Ukraine reflects what is going on and what has been happening in the world over the past several decades. . . . Our western partners, led by the United States of America, prefer not to be guided by international law in their practical policies, but by the rule of the gun. . . . In short, we have every reason to assume that the infamous policy of containment, led in the 18th, 19th and 20th centuries, continues today. They are constantly trying to sweep us into a corner because we have an independent position, because we maintain it and because we call things like they are and do not

There is perhaps no single event that shifted Putin and Russia's view of the United States and the West, nor any definitive period of Russia's changing policy toward the United States, the West, and the U.S.-led international order. Rather, in the immediate post–Cold War period, Russia sought closer relations with the West and even integration into the Western system. From a Russian perspective, the West's reluctance to accept Russia's interests and several Western activities that appeared to threaten those interests increasingly indicated a threat from the West to Russia's interests and security.

Conclusion

The background information presented in this chapter notes key points in the change and continuity in Russian foreign policy and provides the foundation for Russian views of the current international order. There are many other important ideas in Russian political discourse that are sometimes cited as playing a role in its foreign policy, such as a longstanding Russian belief in the importance of power politics,[72] a perception of the need to "catch up" with its rivals,[73] a belief that military power is ultimately decisive over economic power,[74] and a belief that Russia is the defender of conservative values, echoing Samuel Huntington's thesis of a "Clash of Civilizations."[75] The description of Russia's increasing opposition to the U.S.-led order also misses peri-

---

engage in hypocrisy. But there is a limit to everything. And with Ukraine, our western partners have crossed the line, playing the bear and acting irresponsibly and unprofessionally. (Vladimir Putin, "Address by the President of the Russian Federation," March 18, 2014a)

[72] Kuchins and Zevelev, 2012, p. 148; Lilia Shevtsova, "How the West Misjudged Russia, Parts 1–13," *The American Interest*, 2016, Part 2.

[73] Kuchins and Zevelev, 2012, p. 148.

[74] William Zimmerman, Ronald Inglehart, Eduard Ponarin, Yegor Lazarev, Boris Sokolov, Irina Vartanova, and Yekaterina Turanova, *Russian Elite—2020: Valdai Discussion Club Grantees Analytic Report*, Moscow: Valdai International Discussion Club, July 2013, p. 23.

[75] Author discussions with U.S. analysts, Washington, D.C., April 2016; Trenin, 2011, p. 209. See Samuel Huntington, "The Clash of Civilizations?" *Foreign Affairs*, Summer 1993.

ods and areas of increased and potential cooperation with the United States. The next chapter explores in more detail Russia's current view of the international order and its approach to specific components of that order, offering more nuance and detail in Russia's approach to specific institutions. The principles outlined in this chapter and the broad trajectory of Russia's foreign policy explain, to a great extent, how Russian leadership sees the current international order.

CHAPTER THREE

Russian Views of the Current International Order and Its Components

We examine Russian views of the current international order in two parts. First, we examine Russia's views of the underlying logic of the order—namely, how it sees major rules, norms, and institutions influencing state behavior in the current international environment. In brief, Russia sees the logic of the current order as U.S.-led hegemony, in which the United States seeks to bring more countries in the world under its control and influence under the guise of expanding democracy and free institutions.

Second, we detail Russia's perspectives, policies, and behaviors toward the following six major components of the international order:

1. the UN system and related multilateral agreements
2. multilateral regional security agreements (such as NATO and the CSTO)
3. regional organizations (such as the EU and Eurasian Customs Union)
4. multilateral international economic institutions (such as the WTO, Group of Seven [G-7], and International Monetary Fund [IMF])[1]
5. arms control and related multilateral security agreements (such as the nonproliferation regime)
6. general norms of sovereignty, democracy, and human rights.

---

[1] The G-7 includes Canada, France, Germany, Italy, Japan, the United Kingdom, and the United States.

While the overarching negative view of the order's logic carries over to these components to some degree, there is considerable variability in Russian sentiments toward the various components. Where Russia sees the potential for cooperation in ways that would respect its position as a great power and promote security in its region, it is eager for cooperation; where Russia sees the potential for a component of the order to threaten its interests, it generally opposes U.S. policy.

Current Views of the International Order

Russian leaders and analysts currently articulate a view that the U.S.-led order is expanding to encompass the entire world, thereby threatening the security of Russia and its neighbors and undermining Russian influence in its near abroad. According to this view, the West's perception of its own superior power has led it to overreach. Activities that the West claims will bring freedom and democracy, such as Western military intervention and support for civil society, instead increasingly threaten Russian security and its vital interests.

Putin has explained at length his views of the U.S.-led order. He describes the current order as unipolarity and claims that it does not reflect the real balance of power—and, hence, U.S. policy poses significant dangers. In his 2007 speech in Munich, Putin described unilateral action as "not only unacceptable but also impossible in today's world."[2] He also noted that "we are witnessing an almost uncontained hyper use of force—military force—in international relations" and specifically observed that the United States "has overstepped its national borders in every way."[3] His subsequent speeches and discussions include similar rhetoric.[4] In Putin's view, U.S.-led activity is especially prob-

---

[2] Putin, 2007.

[3] Putin, 2007.

[4] For example, in a 2012 newspaper article, Putin highlighted the threat of the United States and NATO to stability:

> I think that indivisible security for all nations, unacceptability of the disproportionate use of force, and unconditional compliance with the fundamental principles of interna-

lematic because the U.S. approach does not reflect current distribution of power. For example, he explained in 2014,

> Pardon the analogy, but this is the way nouveaux riches behave when they suddenly end up with a great fortune, in this case, in the shape of world leadership and domination. Instead of managing their wealth wisely, for their own benefit too of course, I think they have committed many follies.[5]

Lavrov similarly highlights the hypocrisy of Western activities. In a March 2016 article, he writes, "We see how the United States and the U.S.-led Western alliance are trying to preserve their dominant positions by any available method or, to use the American lexicon, ensure their 'global leadership.'" He also describes the diverse methods through which the United States pursues its political goals, including "economic sanctions," "direct armed intervention," "large-scale information wars," and "unconstitutional change of governments." Citing Putin, he writes that the EU and NATO are treading on the freedom of their new member states, because "representatives of these countries concede behind closed doors that they can't take any significant decision without the green light from Washington or Brussels."[6]

Russian analysts have also warned of the universalist and threatening character of Western activities. Alexander Lukin, a Russian Sinologist, identifies a Western philosophy of "'democratism,' a one-sided mixture of political liberalism, human-rights thinking, Enlightenment secularism and theories of Western supremacy that strongly

---

tional law are indispensable postulates. Any neglect of these norms destabilizes the world situation. It is in this light that we view certain aspects of US and NATO activities that do not follow the logic of modern development and are based on the stereotypes of bloc mentality. (Putin, 2012)

Similarly, at a meeting of the Valdai International Discussion Club in 2014, he noted, "In a situation where you had domination by one country and its allies, or its satellites rather, the search for global solutions often turned into an attempt to impose their own universal recipes" (Putin, 2014b).

[5]   Putin, 2014b.

[6]   Sergey Lavrov, "Russia's Foreign Policy: Historical Background," *Russia in Global Affairs*, March 5, 2016.

resembled colonialism." According to Lukin's description, the West believes that "the best way to introduce the 'backward' nations of the world to the joys of freedom and democracy is to incorporate them into Western-dominated economic and political alliances."[7] Fyodor Lukyanov highlights and questions the effectiveness of attempts by the United States to create a unipolar world—that is, "'a new world order' in which Western countries had not only a political but also a moral right to organize the world as they saw fit."[8] Lukyanov is skeptical about the ability of the current system of international institutions to adapt to changes in the balance of power,[9] yet he does not offer a clear solution.[10]

Russian analysts also emphasize the development of competing powers—especially China—and new institutions to replace the current system. Lukin highlights how Russia and other rising powers, including the BRICS countries, share interests beyond objecting to Western universal demands; such interests include strengthening international institutions to reflect shared goals of domestic noninterference.[11] Similarly, Andrei Bezrukov and Andrei Sushentsov at the Moscow State

---

[7]   Lukin, 2016, p. 94.

[8]   Lukyanov, 2016a.

[9]   Lukyanov writes, "The international system sank into chaos as its institutions—reasonably effective in the last century, but unable to adapt to new-century realities—eroded. Attempts to create a 'centralized' or unipolar global system of governance simply failed" (Lukyanov, 2016a). In another article, he observes that there are simply "too many mid-range countries seeking to make [the international system] into the international premier league" (Fyodor Lukyanov, "The World in 2015: A Nostalgia for Balance," *Russia in Global Affairs*, December 24, 2015).

[10]   He writes, "[T]he era that began with the end of the Cold War has ended. For the West, that era was marked by the euphoria of victory. For Russia, it was felt via the sting of inferiority that came from strategic defeat. Both sensations led to a dead end, and there is no way out in sight—even if such an exit will have to be found urgently" (Lukyanov, 2016a).

[11]   Lukin further writes,

> Russia's refusal to follow the Western course is only the first sign of conflict between the West's united-world project and an emerging multipolar system. In a multipolar world, the influence of the West will diminish, while that of other centres of power (China, India, Brazil) will grow as they seek to build zones of influence around their borders. (Lukin, 2016, p. 109)

Institute of International Relations (MGIMO) write, "As a result of universal globalization and emancipation, the organizations that set the rules of the game in the economic and security sectors—the World Bank, the [IMF], and the UN Security Council—do not reflect the real balance of power."[12] However, there remains a great deal of uncertainty in Russian accounts of how the new order will look. The Valdai Discussion Club Report of 2016, for example, envisions the development of two main groupings in the world, one including "the USA, the European Union, and their allies," and the second including "China, Russia, and a number of other countries supporting them."[13] The report notes the potential synergies between Russia's military and China's economic power while downplaying the risk of conflict over Central Asia, but there remains uncertainty about whether the relationship between Russia and China will be cooperative.[14]

The unifying theme of these accounts is that, from a Russian perspective, the fundamental logic of the current international order is the dominance of the United States. Where the United States seeks to gain allied consent and collaboration and where it claims to work on the basis of rules, norms, and institutions independent of U.S. agency, Russian leaders and analysts see, and are concerned about, U.S. control over its allies and manipulation of global institutions. That does not mean that Russia is opposed to the existing major institutions; indeed, as we will see later, Russia continues to see the possibility of adapting several components of the international order to reflect its interests rather than U.S. domination.

---

[12] Andrei Bezrukov and Andrei Sushentsov, "Contours of an Alarming Future," *Russia in Global Affairs*, No. 3, September 2015.

[13] Oleg Barabanov, Timofey Bordachev, Fyodor Lukyanov, Andrey Sushentsov, Dmitry Suslov, and Ivan Timofeev, *War and Peace in the 21st Century: International Stability and Balance of the New Type*, Moscow: Valdai International Discussion Club, January 21, 2016, p. 8.

[14] Barabanov et al., 2016, pp. 8–12.

Russian Views of Components of the International Order

The United Nations System and Related Multilateral Agreements

Russian leaders are supportive of the UN system because it fulfills several of Russia's key objectives. The system grants Russia recognition as a great power through permanent membership and veto power on the Security Council. It also offers a platform to prevent, or at least delegitimize, both noninterference in domestic affairs where Russia does not approve and a coordinated international response to Russia's own interventions. Russia also uses the UN system to protect secondary interests, such as pursuing an interpretation of information security friendly to Russian interests and helicopter sales to UN peace missions.[15]

Russian officials have frequently cited the UN when questioning U.S. policies that, in their view, violate the sovereignty of UN member states. Before the outbreak of hostilities in Kosovo in January 1999, Foreign Minister Igor Ivanov stated that U.S. use of force outside of a UN Security Council resolution was "fraught with the danger of undermining the existing system of international relations."[16] Similarly, as discussed later, Russian leaders criticized both the failure to pass a UN resolution preceding the U.S.-led interventions in Iraq and U.S. actions in Libya for exceeding the UN mandate.

Just before returning to the presidency in 2012, Putin emphasized the value of the UN, implicitly referencing concerns about the United States by stating that it was important for the "United Nations and its Security Council to effectively counter the dictates of some countries and their arbitrary actions in the world arena" and adding, "Nobody has the right to usurp the prerogatives and powers of the U.N., particularly the use of force against sovereign nations."[17] President Putin's chief of staff, Sergey Ivanov, echoed a similar argument in 2015 in an interview with government-run news agency TASS, in which he highlighted how Western unilateral action undermined "universally rec-

---

[15] Author discussions with U.S. officials, Washington, D.C., April 2016.

[16] Igor Ivanov and Madeleine K. Albright, "Joint Press Conference," Moscow, January 26, 1999.

[17] Putin, 2012.

ognized institutions, like the UN Security Council."[18] Russia's official documents also affirm the importance of the UN, including the 2013 Foreign Policy Concept:

> The United Nations should remain the center for regulation of international relations and coordination in world politics in the 21st century, as it has proven to have no alternative and also possesses unique legitimacy. Russia supports the efforts aimed at strengthening the UN's central and coordinating role.[19]

Russian leaders' belief in the UN system is noticeable through Russia's continued use of the UN as a framework for discussion even when there is conflict and disagreement with the other world powers. Figure 3.1 shows Russia's speeches in the UN General Assembly and the number of U.S. speeches for comparison. Even when there were periods of friction between Russia's actions and the international order, such as in Georgia in 2008 and in Ukraine in 2014, Russian officials continued to use the UN as a platform for discussion, if not necessarily agreement or compromise.[20] Accounts of Russia's behavior in the UN emphasize that Russia has no problem using apparently contradictory rhetoric on different issues—for example, using U.S. support for Kosovo's independence to justify its action in Crimea while still opposing independence for Kosovo. Further, Russia is able to compartmentalize policies on different issues, effectively approaching its interests within the UN without being constrained by a single, overarching ideology.[21] Russia has sporadically used its veto power on the Security Council, but never more than twice in any year. However, because knowledge of Russia's intent to veto sometimes prevented resolutions from reach-

---

[18] Sergey Ivanov, "Don't Think the Kremlin Always Decides Everything, Sometimes It Doesn't," TASS Russian News Agency, October 19, 2015.

[19] Ministry of Foreign Affairs of the Russian Federation, 2013.

[20] There are limits to what can be inferred from simply the number of speeches, and it may be useful for other work to more fully analyze the content and apparent intent of these speeches.

[21] Author discussions with U.S. officials, Washington, D.C., April 2016.

Figure 3.1
Number of Speeches in the United Nations General Assembly, Russia and the United States, 1993–2015

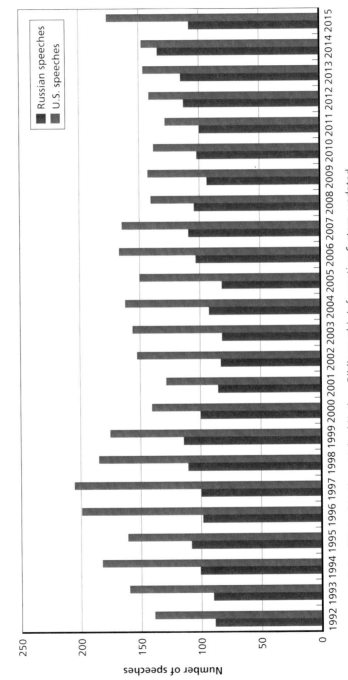

SOURCE: RAND analysis of United Nations, United Nations Bibliographic Information System, undated.

RAND RR1826-3.1

ing a vote, Russian vetoes are, at best, a limited indicator of changes in Russia's behavior.

Overall, Russia supports the UN system, but this support seems to stem mainly from the UN's recognition of Russia's great-power status and its veto power on the UN Security Council. This veto gives Russia the ability to limit Western interference in its own region and prevent a UN response to Russia's own interventions, such as in Crimea. Russia's behavior within the UN is often in opposition with U.S. interests— for example, when Russia vetoed accepting Kosovo's independence and blocked a resolution condemning its behavior in Crimea. Nevertheless, Russia's support for the UN aligns, in many ways, with U.S. goals of maintaining the UN as an integral part of the international order.

Multilateral Regional Security Agreements

NATO and NATO enlargement represent one of the principal points of contestation between the United States and Russia. While the United States emphasizes that NATO is not intended to threaten Russia and sees NATO as a major tool to ensure stability, security, and democratic values,[22] Russian officials and analysts have increasingly seen NATO and NATO enlargement as a threat to Russia's security. Russian fears about NATO enlargement reflect both real concerns about losing influence in its near abroad and paranoia of a NATO invasion facilitated by NATO's growing military presence on Russia's borders. To counter NATO's influence, Russia has sought to develop pan-European, multilateral security arrangements in which it is respected as a great power and to strengthen competing security institutions, such as the CSTO, among the post-Soviet states.

Russian leaders point to discussions between Gorbachev and U.S. Secretary of State James Baker in 1990 to claim that the United States and NATO reneged on a promise not to expand NATO eastward. According to one account of the discussions, Baker assured Gorbachev and Soviet Foreign Minister Eduard Schevardnadze that "there will be no extension of NATO's jurisdiction or NATO's forces one inch to the

---

[22] U.S. Mission to NATO, "Why NATO Matters," Brussels, undated.

East."[23] Mark Kramer, however, writes that these discussions focused on the status of East Germany, and therefore "no Western leader ever offered any 'pledge' or 'commitment' or 'categorical assurances' about NATO's role vis-à-vis the rest of the Warsaw Pact countries."[24] There does not appear to have been a written guarantee about no further expansion of NATO. Nevertheless, the status of Poland and other countries was under discussion during the negotiations between Baker and Gorbachev, and Russian leaders understood Baker, in the context of a more positive U.S.-Russian dialogue at the end of the Cold War, as implying that the United States would not enlarge NATO further east.[25] Shifrinson notes that U.S. "efforts throughout 1990 to engage the Soviet Union implied the existence of a non-expansion deal; as Gorbachev subsequently noted, assurances against NATO expansion were part of the 'spirit' of the 1990 debates."[26] Baker emphasized themes important to the Soviet Union and subsequently Russia in May 1990, including that the United States was "committed to building the pan-European security institutions desired by the Soviet Union," would not seek a "unilateral advantage," and would build "a differ-

---

[23] Shifrinson, 2016, p. 15.

[24] Mark Kramer, "The Myth of a No-NATO-Enlargement Pledge to Russia," *Washington Quarterly*, Vol. 32, No. 2, April 2009, p. 41.

[25] Baker noted in one discussion,

> All our allies and East Europeans we have spoken to have told us that they want us to maintain a presence in Europe. I am not sure whether you favor that or not. . . . We understand the need for assurances to the countries in the East. If we maintain a presence in a Germany that is a part of NATO, there would be no extension of NATO's jurisdiction for forces of NATO one inch to the east." ("Declassified Cable: Memorandum of Conversation Between James A. Baker, Mikhail Gorbachev, and Eduard Shevardnadze at the Kremlin," Washington, D.C.: U.S. Department of State, February 9, 1990, p. 6)

Further, Baker discussed future enlargement of NATO with West German Foreign Minister Hans-Dietrich Genscher in 1990 and subsequently indicated his support for Genscher's position that "NATO would not extend its territorial coverage to the area of the GDR [German Democratic Republic, or East Germany] nor anywhere else in Eastern Europe" (Shifrinson, 2016, p. 22).

[26] Shifrinson, 2016, p. 34.

ent kind of NATO."[27] While neither side had fully conceived of or expected NATO enlargement into eastern Europe in the early 1990s, and hence no formal agreement was made, the negotiations clearly led to a belief among the Russians that the United States was committed to building a new security order that fulfilled core Russian interests.[28]

Later, the Clinton administration adopted a policy of NATO enlargement to avoid the renationalization of defense in Central Europe, promote collective security, and strengthen the European Union, which also set out on a path of enlargement. The aspirant Central and Eastern European members of NATO, as well as some of their supporters in the United States, also saw NATO expansion as a safeguard against a potential future downturn in Russia's relations with the West.[29] Initially, Yeltsin appeared willing to consider NATO enlargement, articulating a rare example of Russian respect for the sovereignty of its neighbors. In August 1993, he stated that Poland had the right to join NATO if it would not conflict with Russian security, explaining, "In the new Russian-Polish relationship, there is no place for hegemony and one state dictating to another."[30] Despite Yeltsin's caveat about Russia's security, this declaration surprised Russian officials, who claimed that Yeltsin must have been drunk and or that it was his "private opinion."[31]

Russian officials during Yeltsin's tenure came to strongly oppose NATO enlargement. There was strong domestic pressure within Russia

---

[27] Shifrinson, 2016, p. 30.

[28] In a January 2016 interview, Putin quoted Egon Bahr, a German politician:

"If we do not now undertake clear steps to prevent a division of Europe, this will lead to Russia's isolation." Bahr, a wise man, had a very concrete suggestion as to how this danger could be averted: the USA, the then Soviet Union and the concerned states themselves should redefine a zone in Central Europe that would not be accessible to NATO with its military structures. Bahr even said: If Russia agreed to the NATO expansion, he would never come to Moscow again. (Nikolaus Blome, Kai Diekmann, and Daniel Biskup, "Putin—The Interview: 'For Me, It Is Not Borders That Matter,'" *Bild*, January 11, 2016)

[29] Talbott, 2002.

[30] Talbott, 2002, pp. 95–96.

[31] Talbott, 2002, p. 96.

against enlargement, especially from Communist and nationalist candidates. During the campaign, Russia's then–Prime Minister Viktor Chernomyrdin told U.S. Vice President Al Gore, "I understand that the decision [on enlargement] has been made, and we know you can't reverse it. But we need help on managing our own domestic politics on the issue."[32] Ronald Asmus notes that at a meeting in early 1997, "Russian communist party head Gennady Zyuganov noted smugly that whereas in Washington there still appeared to be a range of views on enlargement, in Moscow there was only one view—everyone was opposed."[33] Further, Russian media at the time reported opposition from Yeltsin's advisers, who warned, "If NATO moves eastward, Russia will move westward."[34]

By the late 1990s, many senior Russian officials began to perceive that the United States was proceeding with NATO enlargement, with or without their support. In response, they effectively adopted a dual-track policy in which they simultaneously voiced opposition to NATO and agreed to the NATO-Russia Founding Act to secure Russia's interests.[35] The act included the creation of the NATO-Russia Permanent Joint Council, which offered symbolic recognition to Russia as a counterpart to NATO; the statement that NATO members had "no intention, no plan, and no reason to deploy nuclear weapons" on the

---

[32] Talbott, 2002, p. 233.

[33] Ronald D. Asmus, *Opening NATO's Door*, New York: Columbia University Press, 2002, p. 181.

[34] Asmus, 2002, p. 182.

[35] As Asmus recounts,

> On the one hand, [Russian Foreign Minister] Primakov continued to tell Washington that Moscow valued U.S.-Russian cooperation and wanted to work closely to build a new cooperative NATO-Russia relationship. [Russian Deputy Foreign Minister] Mamedov was claiming that Moscow realized that enlargement was going to happen and he had been authorized to "brainstorm" with Talbott on what such a relationship might look like. On the other hand, Primakov continued to attack NATO enlargement, warn of its destabilizing consequences, and probe Washington's European allies for signs of division and weakness. Mamedov's counterpart in the Russian Foreign Ministry responsible for European affairs, Deputy Foreign Minister Nikolai Afan'evsky, was touring European capitals with a tougher message and a long laundry list of Russian demands designed to tie NATO in knots. (Asmus, 2002, p. 172)

territory of the new member states; and a statement that the alliance would not permanently station additional substantial combat forces in Europe "in the current and foreseeable security environment."[36] NATO began to admit candidate countries, with Poland, the Czech Republic, and Hungary joining in 1999 and the Baltic countries—Romania, Slovakia, and Slovenia—joining in 2004.

The negotiations between Clinton and Yeltsin demonstrate the conflict between Russia's goals of establishing cooperation as an equal partner and its interest in protecting its sphere of influence. At a meeting with Clinton in March 1997, Yeltsin noted, "Our position has not changed. It remains a mistake for NATO to move eastward. . . . I am prepared to enter into an agreement not because I want to but because it's a step I'm compelled to take."[37] Yeltsin sought specifically to oppose the accession of the former Soviet republics, including the Baltic states, into NATO. Clinton responded that singling out countries would undermine the idea that NATO was an inclusive security organization that might one day include Russia. By opposing NATO enlargement in a few countries, Russia would demonstrate that it was indeed threatening to the eastern European countries and would thereby reinforce NATO's role of defending Europe against Russia. Nevertheless, statements from Eastern European countries, and informal opinions from U.S. leaders, made clear that a major purpose of NATO was precisely to defend those countries from Russia, dampening U.S. rhetoric about the creation of a dramatically new security community.[38]

---

[36] More precisely, "NATO reiterates that in the current and foreseeable security environment, the Alliance will carry out its collective defence and other missions by ensuring the necessary interoperability, integration, and capability for reinforcement rather than by additional permanent stationing of substantial combat forces" (NATO, "Founding Act on Mutual Relations, Cooperation and Security Between NATO and the Russian Federation, Signed in Paris, France," May 27, 1997).

[37] Talbott, 2002, p. 238.

[38] For example, in 1993, early discussions between Clinton and the leaders of Poland, the Czech Republic, and Hungary emphasized the desire to see NATO enlargement for defense against Russia. Asmus writes that the leaders of these countries "had a common view. Their countries were vulnerable. They still feared Russia. They did not trust the major West European powers. They trusted America" (Asmus, 2002, p. 23). See also Mankoff, 2009, p. 153.

Although Russian leaders, at times, appeared to accept or at least tolerate NATO enlargement,[39] they ultimately developed a conventional wisdom that NATO enlargement was a threat to Russian interests, especially to Russia's influence in its near abroad. U.S. leaders attempted to convince Russia that NATO was not a threat and would respect Russian interests by offering Russia the possibility of joining the Alliance. The prospect of joining Western institutions was attractive to Russian officials so long as Russia was respected as a great power; Russian leaders expected "something like a co-chairmanship of the Western club," as Trenin writes.[40] However, for NATO, "the door to the West would remain open, but the idea of Russia's actually entering through it remained unthinkable"[41] absent major changes in Russia's governing institutions and, most likely, in Western politics.[42]

---

[39] In his 2005 address to the Federal Assembly, Putin simply stated, "We hope that the new members of NATO and the European Union in the post-Soviet area will show their respect for human rights, including the rights of ethnic [Russian] minorities, through their actions" (Putin, 2005). Furthermore, as Trenin writes,

> On the issue of NATO enlargement, Moscow would be wise to leave the decisions to the countries in question. Whether candidate countries join the Alliance—and if so, when—should be up to those nations themselves. In view of Moscow's stated goals, Russian intervention can only be counterproductive. The Kremlin's official position of treating Alliance accession as a sovereign right of each individual country, and of focusing on the management of Russia's own security, makes good sense. It may be that Georgia will get the Membership Action Plan in the spring of 2008, which would put the country on track to join the Alliance a few years later. In Ukraine, however, NATO must admit that the accession issue is likely to remain politically divisive and potentially destabilising. Calm handling of these situations by both sides would help to uphold stability and security in Europe's east. (Dmitri Trenin, "NATO and Russia: Sobering Thoughts and Practical Suggestions," *NATO Review*, Summer 2007)

[40] Trenin, 2006.

[41] Trenin, 2006.

[42] Henry Kissinger, for example, opposed possible Russian membership in NATO, writing in 2001, "But Russian membership in NATO—however partial—is not the solution. NATO is, and remains, basically a military alliance, part of whose purpose is the protection of Europe against Russian invasion" (Henry Kissinger, "Russia a Partner, but Not in NATO," *Washington Post*, December 7, 2001). Instead, drawing a connection to the Concert of Europe, he noted,

> Russia should become a full and equal partner in political discussions affecting international order. On matters affecting Atlantic relations, the consultative machinery of the

The practical rejection of Russia's accession hardened Russian views toward Western institutions by demonstrating that Russia could not be integrated and, therefore, that NATO would continue to appear in opposition to Russia.

Russian opposition intensified as NATO pursued the integration of new members and as it became clear to Russian officials that the institutions to include Russia in NATO decisionmaking would not grant Russia significant influence in that decisionmaking. In 2007, Putin described NATO enlargement as "a serious provocation that reduces the level of mutual trust" and expressed concern about NATO bases on Russia's border.[43] In 2008, following the declaration at the Bucharest Summit that Ukraine and Georgia "will become members of NATO," Russia undertook a military campaign in Georgia.[44] According to Hill and Gaddy, "Putin assumed that the shock of Russia's war with Georgia would force a reassessment of U.S. democracy-promotion policies and a recalculation in Washington about how far to go in pushing NATO membership for Georgia and Ukraine."[45] In a 2016 article, Lavrov writes that the choice to pursue NATO enlargement "is the essence of the systemic problems that have soured Russia's relations with the United States and the European Union."[46]

Since the Ukraine crisis, Russian officials have become more explicit in identifying NATO as a threat to Russia. CNA senior

---

Organization for Security and Cooperation in Europe could be raised to the head-of-state level; for global issues, the G-8 [Group of Eight] meetings of industrial democracies could be returned to their original emphasis on substance by giving them a political and not simply an economic subject matter. (Kissinger, 2001)

On the Concert of Europe, see also Kyle Lascurettes, *The Concert of Europe and Great-Power Governance Today: What Can the Order of 19th-Century Europe Teach Policymakers About International Order in the 21st Century?* Santa Monica, Calif.: RAND Corporation, PE-226-OSD, 2017, which is part of the Building a Sustainable International Order series.

[43] Putin, 2007.

[44] NATO, "Bucharest Summit Declaration," April 3, 2008.

[45] Hill and Gaddy, 2013, p. 309.

[46] Lavrov, 2016.

researcher Dmitri Gorenburg paraphrases Valery Gerasimov, the current Chief of the General Staff of Russia's military:

> The most significant threat facing Russia, in Gerasimov's view, comes from NATO. In particular, he highlights the threat from NATO enlargement to the east, noting that all 12 new members added since 1999 were formerly either members of the Warsaw Pact or Soviet republics. This process is continuing, with the potential future inclusion of former Yugoslav republics and continuing talk of perspective Euroatlantic integration of Ukraine and Georgia.[47]

Russia's official documents, including its December 2015 National Security Strategy,[48] also emphasize the growing threat from NATO. Thus, if NATO pursues the further integration of former Soviet countries, Russian officials will likely continue to perceive NATO as aggressive.

As an alternative to NATO, Russia supports the development of strengthened regional security arrangements in which it would have a greater influence. In the early 1990s, Russia advocated the transformation and elevation of the CSCE, with the goal of creating a pan-European institution that improved cooperation with the West while maintaining Russia's prerogatives and interests in its region. The CSCE developed out of negotiations in the 1970s that involved both the Eastern and Western blocs. These negotiations also led to the 1975 Helsinki Final Act, which established such shared principles as territorial integrity and respect for human rights. Following the end of the Soviet Union, Russia continued to support the CSCE, which

---

[47] Dmitry Gorenburg, "Moscow Conference on International Security 2015 Part 2: Gerasimov on Military Threats Facing Russia," Russian Military Reform blog, Cambridge, Mass., May 4, 2015.

[48] The National Security Strategy notes,

> A determining factor in relations with NATO is still the unacceptability for the Russian Federation of the alliance's increased military activity and the approach of its military infrastructure toward Russia's borders, the building of a missile-defense system, and attempts to endow the bloc with global functions executed in violation of the provisions of international law. (Russian Federation, *National Security Strategy*, December 31, 2015)

became the OSCE in 1995.[49] Russian leaders preferred the OSCE over NATO because Russia would retain veto power and have a larger say in the organization's behavior within its near abroad. Indeed, while the OSCE has been active in Bosnia, Kosovo, and Ukraine, its freedom of action has been limited by Russia's veto over its activities.[50]

The OSCE has remained part of Russia's thinking about the international order, and Russia continues to seek either a larger role for the OSCE or the creation of another body that would manage European security and over which Russia would have veto power. In 2010, Lavrov criticized Western countries for preferring NATO enlargement over the elevation of the OSCE:

> When the Soviet Union and the Warsaw Pact ceased to exist, there was a real chance to make the OSCE into a full-fledged organization capable of ensuring equal security for all states in the Euro-Atlantic area. This opportunity was missed, however, as the choice was made in favor of the policy of NATO enlargement, *which in practice meant not only the preservation of the lines dividing Europe into zones with different levels of security, but also the movement of these lines to the East.* . . . Everyone needs security . . . which must be built largely through a universal feeling of equal and equally guaranteed security.[51]

---

[49] Wolfgang Zellner notes that Russia's strategy was largely a carryover from the Soviet period:

> The basic Soviet objectives for the CSCE consisted in securing Western acceptance of the political status quo in Europe, enlarging trade opportunities, and improving access to Western technology, while the USSR [Union of Soviet Socialist Republics] also hoped that the Conference might help emphasise the "Europeanness" of the Soviet Union, while, if possible, reducing the influence of the United States. (Wolfgang Zellner, "Russia and the OSCE: From High Hopes to Disillusionment," *Cambridge Review of International Affairs*, Vol. 18, No. 3, 2005, p. 390)

[50] Zellner identifies two conflicting Russian visions of the OSCE. Russia saw the organization both "as an instrument for fostering Russia's integration into European structures" yet, at the same time, had the objective to "secure a maximum of freedom of action and to avoid Western and, in particular, OSCE intervention in post-Soviet states and, of course, Russia proper" (Zellner, 2005, p. 391).

[51] Lavrov, 2010, emphasis added.

Increasing the role for the OSCE appears to remain popular with Putin, who at his speech at Valdai lauded the OSCE and its role in Ukraine.[52] Medvedev and Lavrov have also offered an alternative or supplement to the OSCE, proposing a new "region-wide" or "comprehensive" European security framework in which Russia would be equally represented, such as a new European Security Treaty.[53]

Partly in response to NATO, Russia has also increasingly developed security institutions in its own region—namely, the CIS and the CSTO. The CIS, which contains all of the former Soviet states except the Baltic countries, was originally intended to manage the divorce of its members from the Soviet Union. Analysts highlight that the CIS's capabilities are limited.[54] Instead, especially following the Georgian war in 2008, Russia has focused greater effort on developing the CSTO, apparently intending both to mirror NATO and to balance against it.[55] After doing little to develop the CSTO in the early 2000s, Russia encouraged the development of a rapid-reaction force within the CSTO and, in the early 2010s, continued to develop the organization's ability to conduct peace missions.[56] Russia continues to pursue military exercises within the framework of the CSTO and has taken actions to develop a unified command structure. However, Russian leadership over the CSTO has been undermined by Russia's unwillingness to take sides in the local conflicts of the member states.[57]

---

[52] Putin, 2014b.

[53] Richard Weitz, *The Rise and Fall of Medvedev's European Security Treaty*, Washington, D.C.: German Marshall Fund of the United States, May 2012.

[54] See Carol R. Saivetz, "The Ties That Bind? Russia's Evolving Relations with Its Neighbors," *Communist and Post-Communist Studies*, Vol. 45, No. 3–4, 2012, p. 403.

[55] Current CSTO member states include Russia, Armenia, Belarus, Kazakhstan, Kyrgyzstan, and Tajikistan, after Azerbaijan, Uzbekistan, and Georgia left the organization (Matthew Bodner, "With Ukraine Revitalizing NATO, Russia Dusts Off Its Own Security Alliance," *Moscow Times*, October 23, 2014; Saivetz, 2012, p. 403).

[56] International Institute for Strategic Studies, *The Military Balance*, New York: Taylor & Francis Group, March 14, 2013, pp. 208–210; and John Mowchan, *The Militarization of the Collective Security Treaty Organization*, Carlisle, Penn.: Center for Strategic Leadership, U.S. Army War College, Issue Paper, Vol. 6-09, July 2009.

[57] Bodner, 2014.

Although the CSTO and CIS officially recognize the independence and equality of their member states, Russia exercises significant informal influence over these countries, partly through its threat to provoke instability if these countries do not follow Russia's line.[58] One way to understand Russian views of the U.S. relationship with NATO and the EU is through the lens of Russia's relationship with its neighbors. From Russia's point of view, the CSTO, CIS, and Eurasian Economic Union are formal organizations that offer a public front for Russia's influence in its region. In a parallel way, Russian leaders view NATO, and perhaps the EU to a lesser extent, as formal organizations that mask Washington's informal influence.[59]

Regional Organizations

Until 2013, Russia had been generally supportive of the EU and EU integration, although it expressed significant concerns with Europe's failure to treat Russia as a great power. Since 2013, EU enlargement into the former Soviet space, especially integration of Ukraine, Moldova, and Georgia, has provoked significant Russian opposition, including military action in Ukraine. Russia has also supported the development of competing or parallel regional organizations, especially the Eurasian Economic Union, and undertaken a range of political, military, and economic measures to undermine the EU.

As part of Russia's overall policy of improving relations with the West, Yeltsin promised early in the Cold War to do "everything possible to support European integration," and through the 1994 Partnership and Cooperation Agreement, Russia developed formal structures of cooperation with the EU. In 2001, Putin gave a speech in German to the Bundestag, noting, "As for European integration, we not just support these processes, but we are looking to them with hope."[60]

However, Russia's views of the EU changed with the European Neighborhood Policy, which sought to develop a "ring of friends" around the EU and enable its neighbors to participate in "everything

---

[58] Author discussions with U.S. analysts, Washington, D.C., March 2016.

[59] Author discussions with U.S. analysts, Washington, D.C., March 2016.

[60] Putin, 2007.

but institutions."[61] The EU approached Russia to participate in the policy, but only at a level equal to that of other countries in the region, such as Moldova, Ukraine, and Georgia. Following its principle of participation equal to that of great powers, Russia declined. As former Swedish Prime Minister Carl Bildt notes, "Its rejection was less about refusing the details of cooperation and integration, but more about not wanting to be treated in the same framework as what it considered lesser nations, and about a wish to establish more direct and equal relations with the EU."[62] Similarly, Arbatov and Dynkin write, "Russia, the biggest and closest EU neighbour, was put into the same group as the most distant Mediterranean countries. Given Russia's post-imperial complexes and its obsession with status, Moscow's response to the EU offer was predictably negative."[63]

Around 2007 or 2008, Russia began to develop the Eurasian Customs Union as an alternative and competitor to the EU. Prior to this point, Russia had taken measures to develop economic relations with the former Soviet countries through the CIS and a range of bilateral agreements. The depth, breadth, and implementation of these agreements were limited, however, undermining integration, especially because Russia was reluctant to invest substantial resources.[64]

According to one account by a former Russian official, the main impetus for further regional integration came not from Russia but from Kazakhstan. Kazakhstan sought Russia's greater involvement in Central Asia, partly to balance concerns about the rise of China. Although Kazakhstan was at first unsuccessful at getting Russia to launch a new initiative, other factors—including Russia's difficulty in joining the

---

[61] Carl Bildt, *Russia, the European Union, and the Eastern Partnership*, European Council on Foreign Relations, May 19, 2015, p. 3.

[62] Bildt, 2015, p. 3.

[63] Arbatova and Dynkin, 2016, p. 84.

[64] Rilka Dragneva and Joop De Kort, "The Legal Regime for Free Trade in the Commonwealth of Independent States," *International and Comparative Law Quarterly*, Vol. 56, No. 2, April 2007, pp. 236–239; and Rilka Dragneva and Kataryna Wolczuk, *Russia, the Eurasian Customs Union and the EU: Cooperation, Stagnation or Rivalry?* London: Chatham House, August 2012.

WTO and the 2008 financial crisis—led Russia to take a more positive view of building institutions that would compete with and offer an alternative to the West.[65] By 2007, Russia agreed to develop a Customs Union with Kazakhstan and Belarus, which was eventually launched in 2010.[66]

In 2011, in an article in *Izvestia*, Putin articulated that Russia intended to pursue a regional integration process through the Eurasian Customs Union and successor organizations:

> A crucial integration project, the Common Economic Space of Russia, Belarus and Kazakhstan (CES), will kick off on January 1, 2012. . . . By building the Customs Union and Common Economic Space, we are laying the foundation for a prospective Eurasian economic union. At the same time, the Customs Union and CES will expand by involving Kyrgyzstan and Tajikistan. We plan to go beyond that, and set ourselves an ambitious goal of reaching a higher level of integration—a Eurasian Union.[67]

Putin emphasized that the Eurasian Union, like the EU, would be open to other countries and urged the development of relations between the EU and the Eurasian Union in the future as part of a

---

[65] Putin noted in 2011,

It is clear today that the 2008 global crisis was structural in nature. We still witness acute reverberations of the crisis that was rooted in accumulated global imbalances. At the same time, the elaboration of post-crisis global development models is proving to be a difficult process. For example, the Doha Round is virtually mired in stalemate, the WTO faces objective difficulties, and the principle of free trade and open markets is itself in deep crisis. We believe that a solution might be found in devising common approaches from the bottom up, first within the existing regional institutions, such as the EU, [North American Free Trade Agreement], [Asia-Pacific Economic Cooperation], [Association of Southeast Asian Nations] inter alia, before reaching an agreement in a dialogue between them. These are the integration bricks that can be used to build a more sustainable global economy. (Vladimir Putin, "Novyj Integratsionnyj Proyekt Dlya Evrazii: Budushchee, Kotoroe Rozhdaetsya Segodnya [New Integration Project for Eurasia: The Future in the Making]," *Izvestia*, October 3, 2011)

[66] Author discussion with former Russian official, Washington, D.C., April 2016; see also Dragneva and Wolczuk, 2012, p. 4.

[67] Putin, 2011.

goal of developing a continent-wide free trade agreement.[68] At the same time, Putin referenced the goal of building an alternative power center around Russia, noting that the union would become a "powerful supranational association capable of becoming one of the poles in the modern world and serving as an efficient bridge between Europe and the dynamic Asia-Pacific region."[69]

Despite Russian support for the Eurasian Union, scholars and analysts have described it as an "essentially political project" aimed at regional integration. They have downplayed its economic influence or logic, noting that Russia and its partners lack the size and diversity of the countries that went on to form the EU. For example, Russia is significantly larger than any other member, and many of the member states, including Russia, are major exporters of oil, gas, and other commodities, which brings into question the gains of increased economic integration. Further, there are doubts that Russia will indeed seek to develop the Eurasian Union structures into a full-fledged political and economic union.[70] European audiences also view the Eurasian project as challenging to the creation of a single economic space in Europe, because trade from the EU may face barriers in entering the Eurasian Customs Union. Therefore, while Russia may have political reasons to demonstrate the development and effectiveness of the Eurasian Union, it does not appear that the Eurasian Union is likely to become the competitor or alternative to the EU that Russia claims to seek.

In 2012 and 2013, the potential integration of Ukraine, Georgia, Moldova, and Armenia with the EU through the signing of EU Association Agreements and Deep and Comprehensive Free Trade Area agreements led to increasing Russian opposition. In particular,

---

[68] Putin explained,

> Some of our neighbours explain their lack of interest in joining forward-looking integration projects in the post-Soviet space by saying that these projects contradict their pro-European stance. I believe that this is a false antithesis. We do not intend to cut ourselves off, nor do we plan to stand in opposition to anyone. The Eurasian Union will be based on universal integration principles as an essential part of Greater Europe united by shared values of freedom, democracy, and market laws. (Putin, 2011)

[69] Putin, 2011.

[70] Saivetz, 2012, p. 406; Trenin, 2011, p. 155; see also Bildt, 2015, p. 7.

Russia put a great deal of pressure on Ukraine to reverse its decision to proceed with EU integration, including a threat to cut off some trade. In explaining Russian resistance to Ukraine's western integration, Putin has emphasized the likely harm of EU goods flooding the Russian market,[71] and he has argued that Western policy was "not centered on protecting the interests of Ukraine" but instead sought "to disrupt an attempt to recreate the Soviet Union."[72] Russian Deputy Prime Minister Dmitri Rogozin argued at the time that Ukraine's signing of an Association Agreement with the EU was a precursor to eventual NATO membership.[73] Russia similarly pushed the other former Soviet states to reject closer ties with the EU, although only Armenia reversed course and joined the Eurasian Customs Union.[74]

---

[71] At his 2014 address to Valdai, Putin noted,

> Because in implementing Ukraine's association project, our partners would come to us with their goods and services through the back gate, so to speak, and we did not agree to this, nobody asked us about this. We had discussions on all topics related to Ukraine's association with the EU, persistent discussions, but I want to stress that this was done in an entirely civilised manner, indicating possible problems, showing the obvious reasoning and arguments. Nobody wanted to listen to us and nobody wanted to talk. (Putin, 2014b)

See also Sergey Aleksashenko, "For Ukraine, Moldova, and Georgia Free Trade with Europe and Russia Is Possible," Beirut, Lebanon: Carnegie Middle East Center, July 3, 2014.

[72] Vladimir Putin, "Interview on Miroporyadok [World Order]," trans. Clinton Reach, Moscow: Rossiya HD, December 20, 2015b. Hill and Gaddy write,

> In Putin's view the situation that unfolded in Ukraine in 2013–14 reflected as if in a mirror . . . what was happening in the world as a whole. Developments in Ukraine, and the efforts of the European Union to create a new relationship with Ukraine, were simply a continuation, if not the culmination of several decades of efforts by the West to put pressure on Russia and thwart its foreign policy priorities. . . . The West—"our Western partners," as he called them—had crossed a line . . . by pushing Ukraine towards the European Union, just as it had crossed a line in 2008 by promising eventual NATO membership to both Ukraine and Georgia. (Hill and Gaddy, 2013, p. 265)

[73] Aleksashenko, 2014.

[74] Andrew Gardner, "Armenia Chooses Russia over EU," *Politico*, September 3, 2013. It is contested whether Russia intended for its other neighbors to ultimately join Eurasian Union structures as an alternative to the EU. Some analysts argue that Russia did not require that Ukraine join, given the lack of popular support for the Eurasian Union in Ukraine and risk of cheap goods flowing through Ukraine, while others state that Ukraine's accession

After Ukrainian President Viktor Yanukovych indicated his decision not to sign the Association Agreement and its Deep and Comprehensive Free Trade Area agreement, major protests broke out in Maidan Square in Kyiv. These protests contributed to the fall of the Yanukovych government, and Russia responded by annexing Crimea and later supporting the separatist movement in Ukraine.[75] In the context of the Western effort to extend the EU, Russia's annexation of Crimea may have been "a completely reasonable act of self-defense," as Hill and Gaddy report that Putin and other Russian elites believe. Indeed, in a speech in March 2014, shortly after Russia's military action in Crimea, Putin observed, "[The West] must have really lacked political instinct and common sense not to foresee all the consequences of their actions. Russia found itself in a position it could not retreat from. If you compress the spring all the way to its limit, it will snap back hard."[76]

If Russia's annexation of Crimea and its support for separatists in eastern Ukraine are any indication, Russia will likely continue to use a wide range of military, political, and economic tools to block further EU accession and preserve influence in the former Soviet republics. Yet such influence is not the limit of Russia's efforts to undermine or influence the EU. Indeed, as ongoing analysis of Russian activities in Europe indicates, Russia has pursued a wide range of means of influence to achieve its objectives.[77]

Multilateral International Economic Institutions

Since the end of the Cold War, Russia has pursued increased economic cooperation with the EU and the West, although there has been con-

---

to the Eurasian Union was essential for the project. On the crisis, see "Summit of Failure: How the EU Lost Russia over Ukraine," Spiegel International, October 16, 2013; and Nate Schenkkan, "Eurasian Disunion: Why the Union Might Not Survive 2015," Foreign Affairs, December 26, 2014. On Ukraine's status within the Eurasian Union, see Anton Barbashin, "A Eurasian Union No More?" National Interest, April 23, 2014.

[75] Hill and Gaddy, 2013, pp. 360–365; Roy Allison, "Russian 'Deniable' Intervention in Ukraine: How and Why Russia Broke the Rules," International Affairs, Vol. 90, No. 6, November 2014.

[76] Putin, 2014a.

[77] See, for example, Conley et al., 2016.

flict within Russia about the extent to which it should accept liberal policies recommended by Western donors.

Yeltsin initiated a major effort to reform Russia's economy and integrate it into the global economic system. International economic institutions, including the G-7 and IMF, provided significant sums to stabilize the Russian government while demanding that Russia make reforms that were perceived as necessary to achieve a market economy. Following the initial tumultuous reform period, in which Western-led reform was discredited for many Russians, Russian officials generally remained supportive of integrating Russia into Western economic institutions, although there has been occasional hesitation. Russia joined the IMF and World Bank in the spring of 1992 and initially applied to the WTO (at the time called the Global Agreement on Tariffs and Trade) in 1993. Russian officials have especially encouraged Western investment in Russia. Putin, for example, emphasized Russia's interest in "further integration of the Russian economy into the international economy" and openness to foreign investment, especially in the energy sector.[78]

However, Russian support for the WTO has been far more variable since 2000; Russia has pursued membership with the goal of becoming a member of leading international organizations, albeit with skepticism of the Western-led institutions. Anders Åslund notes that shortly after Putin's first election, he made Russia's "early entry [to the WTO] one of his priorities in international politics," apparently due, in part, to business support for Russian membership.[79] Putin supported the reform of the responsible ministries and put in place a team of dedicated reformers to negotiate Russia's WTO accession.[80] When he was reelected in 2004, however, Putin instead pursued a less liberal

---

[78] Putin, 2007.

[79] Anders Åslund, "Russia's Accession to the World Trade Organization," *Eurasian Geography and Economics*, Vol. 48, No. 3, 2007, p. 299.

[80] Indeed, Russian and international estimates indicated that Russia would gain between 0.5 and 1 percent growth in gross domestic product per year from WTO accession (Anders Åslund, "Why Doesn't Russia Join the WTO?" *Washington Quarterly*, Vol. 53, No. 60, April 2010).

policy of "import substitution in tandem with extensive state intervention and protectionism."[81] With the financial crisis in 2008, and Russia's lack of progress with the accession negotiations, Putin's skepticism of the WTO apparently increased. In 2009, in a move that was widely interpreted as undermining or stalling Russia's bid for accession, Putin announced that Kazakhstan, Belarus, and Russia planned to enter the WTO together as a customs union.[82] The Medvedev government, with the apparent approval of Putin, reengaged with the WTO negotiations in 2011 and secured Russia's formal accession in 2012. Since becoming a member, officials and analysts assess Russia's participation as generally productive. For example, Russia has not generally rejected Western proposals out of hand and has provided notification on changing laws and regulations generally according to WTO requirements. Analysts assess that Russia's participation in these organizations is based on a desire to be "taken seriously" and to "be part of the civilized world."[83]

Since beginning his third term as President in 2012, Putin has also pursued an agenda of reducing Russian dependence and vulnerability to the international economy. Russia's efforts to bolster its own resources in order to withstand swings in the global economy were not new. Indeed, Alexey Kudrin, Minister of Finance from 2000 through 2011, used a significant portion of oil and gas revenue to pay down foreign debt with this goal in mind.[84] In 2011 and 2012, Putin appears to have pursued a more intensive approach to reduce Russia's economic dependence by encouraging import substitution, demanding that for-

---

[81] Åslund, 2007, p. 299.

[82] Dominic Fean, *Decoding Russia's WTO Accession*, Institut Français des Relations Internationales Russia/NIS Center, February 2012, p. 10. According to one account, after Russian negotiators pursued continued accession in 2009, the government quickly turned around and withdrew from WTO negotiations based on the increasing view that the WTO was a Western-led organization to which Russia should not "kowtow" (Author discussion with U.S. official, Washington, D.C., March 2016). At the time, Medvedev accused the United States of blocking Russia's accession ("Medvedev: Blocking Russia's WTO Entry," CNN, September 15, 2009).

[83] Author discussions with U.S. officials and Russian analysts, Washington, D.C., March–April 2016.

[84] Alexey Kudrin and Evsey Gurvich, "A New Growth Model for the Russian Economy," *Russian Journal of Economics*, Vol. 1, 2015, pp. 33–34.

eign manufacturers produce locally, and spending more on large industrial programs within Russia.[85] Following Western sanctions of Russia in 2014, Russia has expanded this effort. For example, countersanctions against Western agricultural goods appear partly intended to develop Russia's domestic agricultural industry.[86] However, analysts are skeptical that Russia can achieve significant substitution of domestic production for imports, especially given the relatively small investment to date, Russia's continuing dependence on the export of oil and gas (an estimated 17–25 percent between 2000 and 2011), Russia's poor business climate, and the difficulty the government faces in shifting capital away from unprofitable but politically important state-owned enterprises.[87] Hence, while Russia may seek to reduce its dependence on imports and foreign trade, it will face significant challenges in this effort.

Russia has sought expanded representation for itself and other rising powers in the management of the major international financial institutions. For example, Russia has started to participate with China in institutions that might develop competing structures to the major Western-led financial institutions. In mid-2015, Russia reportedly became the third-largest investor (behind China and India) in the Asian Infrastructure Investment Bank, which has been advertised as a potential rival to the World Bank.[88] Russia has sought reform of the IMF to increase representation for China and other rising powers.[89]

---

[85] Hill and Gaddy, 2013, p. 248.

[86] See, for example, "Two Years On: How Russia's Agricultural Sector Reaps the Benefits of Sanctions," *Sputnik News*, August 7, 2016.

[87] Richard Connolly and Philip Hanson, "Import Substitution and Economic Sovereignty in Russia," Chatham House, June 2016; Keith Crane, Shathi Nataraj, Patrick Johnston, and Gursel Rafig oglu Aliyev, *Russia's Medium-Term Economic Prospects*, Santa Monica, Calif.: RAND Corporation, RR-1468-RC, 2016, p. 6; and Clifford G. Gaddy and Barry W. Ickes, "Putin's Rent Management System and the Future of Addiction in Russia," in Susanne Oxenstierna, ed., *The Challenges of Russia's Politicized Economic System*, Abingdon, Oxon, UK: Routledge, 2015, pp. 28–30.

[88] "Russia Becomes 3rd-Biggest Shareholder in China-Led Development Bank," *Moscow Times*, June 29, 2015.

[89] Steve Gutterman, "Putin Says Russia Seeking IMF Reform, Battling Offshores," Reuters, June 13, 2013.

Another forum in which Russia has expressed its support for an alternative financial infrastructure is the annual BRICS summit. The 2015 BRICS declaration, for example, criticized "the prolonged failure by the United States to ratify the IMF 2010 reform package," which included increasing the voting power of the BRICS nations and other developing countries.[90] A report by the Russian think tank Russian Institute for Strategic Studies went further, noting, "Supported by developing countries, the BRICS group is striving for the rearrangement of the whole global economic architecture including the international trade, foreign exchange and financial relations, foreign investments, control over sources of raw materials, regional markets, and high technologies."[91] While Russian rhetoric around the BRICS remains significant, it may be more significant as a forum for the rising powers to voice their concerns rather than an institution by which they execute shared policy.

Arms Control and Related Multilateral Security Agreements

Russia's negotiation and adoption of arms control follow the constraints of the major foreign policy interests outlined in Chapter Two. Where arms control serves Russia's interests—in protecting its security, its influence in its sphere of influence, or its status as a great power—Russia has pursued such agreements. For example, Russia has supported the Non-Proliferation Treaty, which grants the country special recognition. Where Russia fears that it will be at a disadvantage, it has not hesitated to weaken or question the existing order—for example, when it decided to suspend its participation in the Conventional Forces in Europe (CFE) Treaty in 2007 and to officially withdraw in 2015.

The United States and Soviet Union pursued several waves of arms control negotiations that remain important for Russia's relationship with the United States and the current international order. In the 1970s, the United States and Soviet Union signed agreements limiting,

---

[90] Russian Presidency of the 2015 Ufa Summit, "VII BRICS Summit: 2015 Ufa Declaration," University of Toronto BRICS Information Center, July 9, 2015.

[91] I. Prokofyev, V. Kholodkov, and N. Troshin, "East vs. West: Battle for Reforming the World Economy," *Russian Institute for Strategic Studies*, No. 6, January 2015.

for example, the number of strategic launchers and warheads, as well as the development of anti-ballistic missile (ABM) systems.[92] In the closing years of the Cold War, a second series of treaties were signed, including the Intermediate-Range Nuclear Forces (INF) Treaty, which banned both nuclear and nonnuclear weapons with a range between 500 and 5,500 km; the first Strategic Arms Reduction Treaty (START), limiting warheads, missiles, and bombers; and the CFE Treaty, which set limits on several types of conventional forces across a range of European countries.[93] Yeltsin's government remained supportive of the ongoing arms control negotiations, especially because arms control had the potential to reduce Russia's military expenses at a critical time. His government, with Ukraine, Kazakhstan, and Belarus, signed START II in 1992. However, even in the early 1990s, there was opposition within Russia about furthering arms control with the United States and its allies, demonstrated especially by the refusal of the Russian Duma to ratify START II and disagreement about how to modify the CFE Treaty to reflect the post–Cold War environment.[94]

During Putin's presidency, disagreement with the United States about arms control intensified. While the United States emphasized its interest in further agreements, Russia found U.S. pursuit of ballistic missile defense and its withdrawal from the Anti-Ballistic Missile Treaty to be deeply troubling. Furthermore, Russia remained concerned that NATO enlargement would lead to the increasing presence of NATO forces on its borders.[95] In 2007, for example, Lavrov emphasized that Russia would not engage in "horse trading" over anti-

---

[92] Amy F. Woolf, Paul K. Kerr, and Mary Beth D. Nikitin, *Arms Control and Nonproliferation: A Catalog of Treaties and Agreements*, Washington, D.C.: Congressional Research Service, RL33865, April 13, 2016, pp. 4–6.

[93] Woolf, Kerr, and Nikitin, 2016, p. 38.

[94] Talbott, 2002, pp. 181–183, 271–273, 445–446; Jeffrey D. McCausland, "NATO and Russian Approaches to Adapting the CFE Treaty," *Arms Control Association*, August 1, 1997.

[95] Mankoff notes that senior U.S. officials "argued in a joint open letter to President Clinton that the U.S.-led effort to expand NATO not only jeopardized the future of the arms control regime but would also 'bring Russians to question the entire post–Cold War settlement'" (Mankoff, 2009, p. 155).

missile facilitates in the former Warsaw Pact countries.[96] U.S. officials emphasized that the ABM forces were intended for rogue states, that the forces could not undermine Russia's deterrent, and that Russia and the United States were no longer enemies, but this did little to reassure Russia about NATO's intentions.[97] Russia's concern about ABM systems in former Warsaw Pact countries eventually contributed to Russia's decision to leave the CFE Treaty in 2007. Insistence by the United States that Russia withdraw from Georgia, Moldova, and Transnistria may also have factored into Russia's decision.[98]

Nevertheless, Russia has proved cooperative at times on strategic arms control. In 2002, Russia and the United States agreed on the Strategic Offensive Reductions Treaty (often known as the Moscow Treaty), which limited the number of warheads. In 2011, the New START agreement came into force, requiring substantial reductions in the number of launchers and warheads on both sides. This treaty reestablished a comprehensive system of monitoring and verification, which had lapsed with the first START in 2009. Although the treaty required a reduction in the number of Russian warheads, analysts note that it simultaneously enabled Russia to substantially modernize its nuclear arsenal by reducing the cost of maintaining large numbers of static intercontinental ballistic missiles and pursuing systems that would be less vulnerable to a U.S. attack.[99]

Russia has been supportive of the nonproliferation regime and other nonproliferation negotiations. In 2007, Putin stated, "we are unequivocally in favour of strengthening the regime of non-proliferation. The present international legal principles allow us to develop technologies to manufacture nuclear fuel for peaceful purposes."[100] Russia also played a constructive role in the 2015 nuclear deal with Iran. Participating in the negotiations enabled Russia to pursue several goals, including

---

[96] Mankoff, 2009, pp. 159–160.

[97] Talbott, 2002, pp. 389, 418–419.

[98] Mankoff, 2009, p. 160.

[99] Simon Shuster, "Why Russia Is Rebuilding Its Nuclear Arsenal," *Time*, April 4, 2016.

[100] Putin, 2007.

arguing for the diminished need for missile defense in Europe, securing Russia's role in major international negotiations, and opening a potential market for Russian civilian nuclear technology and Russian weaponry.[101]

Despite the potential interest on both the U.S. and Russian sides for arms control, events in 2015 and 2016 offer diminishing signs about the prospects for new agreements. In June 2015, U.S. officials noted that Russia had failed to address U.S. concerns about a Russian ground-launched cruise missile that would potentially violate the INF Treaty. [102] Russian analysts, in turn, state that Russia does not know which system U.S. officials are discussing and highlight potential U.S. violations of the INF Treaty from armed drones or from cruise missiles that could be launched from ground-based ABM sites.[103] In recent years, U.S. officials have pursued negotiations on confidence-building measures, arms control, and strategic stability with Russia, but to little avail. Russian officials have raised concerns about a range of issues, including missile defense, U.S. conventional precision-guided missiles, and the militarization of outer space.[104] In October 2016, Russia also withdrew from three agreements on nuclear cooperation with the United States, noting continued U.S. sanctions on Russia related to Ukraine. While arms control has the potential to fit Russia's desires for the international order, Russia appears unlikely to agree to new confidence-building measures or arms control based on its increasing perception of threat from the West.

---

[101] President Obama noted, "Putin and the Russian government compartmentalized on this in a way that surprised me, and we would have not achieved this agreement had it not been for Russia's willingness to stick with us and the other P5-plus members in insisting on a strong deal" (David M. Herszenhorn, "Russia Quickly Maneuvers to Capitalize on Iran Nuclear Deal," *New York Times*, July 14, 2015).

[102] Michael R. Gordon, "U.S. Says Russia Failed to Correct Violation of Landmark 1987 Arms Control Deal," *New York Times*, June 5, 2015; Author discussions with U.S. analysts and officials, Washington, D.C., October 2016.

[103] Author discussions with Russian analysts, Washington, D.C., October 2016.

[104] Vladimir Dvorkin, "Wars and Armies: Carte Blanche: A New Treaty of the Extension of START III," *Nezavisimaya Gazeta Online*, August 23, 2016.

General Norms of Sovereignty, Democracy, and Human Rights

From a U.S. perspective, a critical part of the international order is the development of norms related to democracy, sovereignty, and human rights. Mazarr and colleagues, for example, emphasize that in such documents as the National Security Council Report 68 (known as NSC-68), U.S. officials write that the creation of order on the basis of freedom and democracy is an essential element of U.S. interests, because in the absence of U.S. leadership to develop a strong liberal order, alternative forms of order that threaten U.S. interests will emerge.[105] Further, from the U.S. perspective, norms of sovereignty, self-determination, democracy, and human rights go hand in hand: A critical element of sovereignty is giving countries the ability to choose the institutions they prefer to join. Finally, U.S. strategic documents, and the practice of U.S. foreign policy in the 1990s and 2000s, indicate a belief that U.S. use of force is justified when governments fail to fulfill minimum standards for protecting their citizens.[106]

Russian views of the norms of sovereignty, democracy, and human rights are very different. As discussed earlier, Russian officials increasingly view the U.S. pursuit of human rights and democracy as a cover for expanding U.S. influence, as well as a threat to Russia's security and regime. Furthermore, Russia's view of itself as more fully sovereign than other countries and its right to a sphere of influence mean that Russia's interpretation of sovereignty is fundamentally in conflict with the U.S approach to universal rights and the right of countries to pursue their own foreign policy goals. Russian discussion of these norms may at times obscure Russia's actual policy, so we focus on Russia's approach to sovereignty, democracy, and human rights by exploring Russian statements and policy around several telling issues: foreign intervention, color revolutions, and information security.

---

[105] Mazarr et al., 2016, pp. 46–54.

[106] The 2015 U.S. National Security Strategy notes, for example, "Military force, at times, may be necessary to defend our country and allies or to preserve broader peace and security, including by protecting civilians facing a grave humanitarian crisis" (White House, 2015, p. 22).

Foreign Intervention

Russia has developed increasingly skeptical views of U.S.-led foreign intervention. At the same time, Russia has undertaken its own foreign interventions—most notably, the recent intervention in Syria—in line with its view of order described earlier.

In Bosnia, Yeltsin opposed NATO air strikes and, according to Talbott, emphasized Russia standing up to the West and protecting the Serbs as a means to gain domestic political support.[107] Russian opposition to NATO action in Kosovo was significantly stronger. Yeltsin warned, "I told NATO, the Americans, the Germans: Don't push us towards military action. Otherwise, there will be a European war for sure and possibly world war."[108] Invoking the UN Charter, the Russian ambassador to Croatia argued that "with its military intervention against Yugoslavia, NATO is destroying the existing world order."[109] Indeed, Russia and the United States almost did come into conflict after the Russian military attempted to seize the Prishtina International Airport in Kosovo.[110]

In retrospect, some Russian commentators saw NATO action in Kosovo as the beginning of the decline of improved U.S.-Russia relations.[111] The Kosovo crisis indicated that NATO was willing to take military action against Russia's allies—namely, Serbia—and that institutions for incorporating Russian thinking, such as the Permanent Joint Council, were likely to be ignored by NATO in a crisis.[112] This increasingly raised the perception that NATO might intervene in Rus-

---

[107] Talbott, 2002, p. 73.

[108] "Yeltsin Warns of Possible World War over Kosovo," CNN, April 9, 1999.

[109] Eduard Kuzmin, "Interview: In Order to Protect National Dignity, Russia Is Prepared to Use Even Nuclear Weapons," *Jutarnji List*, April 17, 1999.

[110] See Talbott, 2002, Chapter 13.

[111] Arbatov and Dynkin, 2016, p. 84.

[112] Oksana Antonenko writes, "Disappointment among Russia's political and military élites over the gap between NATO's rhetoric and the actual substance of Russia–NATO relations makes it nearly impossible to sustain Russian interest in a 'partnership' with the Alliance" (Oksana Antonenko, "Russia, NATO and European Security After Kosovo," *Survival: Global Politics and Strategy*, Vol. 41, No. 4, Winter 1999, p. 125).

sia's sphere of influence without its permission and thereby threaten its core interests.

While Russia opposed the Iraq War, it did not identify the war as a threat to itself or its neighborhood at the time. Russia vetoed the UN resolution authorizing the Iraq War, joining France and Germany in its opposition. Vladimir P. Lukin, a former Russian ambassador to the United States, explained Russia's decision using similar language as European opponents of the war, noting at the time,

> There is a principle here, a basic principle, that if someone tries to wage war on their own account, without other states, without an international mandate, it means all the world is confusion and a wild jungle. . . . Do you know the difference between a policeman and a gangster? A policeman complies with rules that are elaborated not by the policeman, but a certain democratic community accepted by everyone. A gangster implements his own rules.[113]

Major-General G. A. Berezkin, deputy chief of the Russian Ministry of Defense's Central Institute of Military-Technical Information, voiced a stronger critique, writing,

> The military operation of the coalition forces of the U.S. and Great Britain against Iraq in March–April of 2003, to a significant extent is accelerating the formation of an essentially new system of international relations. It is becoming obvious that a significant portion of the global community is yielding to Washington's pressure, which is taking active measures toward radically reshaping the world in its own image.[114]

Nevertheless, Russian rhetoric on the war at the time did not appear to connect U.S. actions to a threat against Russia.

---

[113] John Tagliabue, "France and Russia Ready to Use Veto Against Iraq War," *New York Times*, March 6, 2003.

[114] G.A. Berezkin, "Lessons and Conclusions from the War in Iraq," *Voyennaya Mysl* [*Military Thought*], July 11, 2003, pp. 58–78.

Subsequently, Russian commentators and officials began to connect Kosovo, Iraq, and Libya as part of a more systemic threat to Russian interests and framed these conflicts as a pattern of U.S. activities violating the rules of the international order. In October 2015, Foreign Minister Lavrov argued that humanitarian intervention and the responsibility to protect were not in line with the principles of the UN.[115] In his 2014 speech at the Valdai International Discussion Club's annual meeting, Putin voiced sarcasm that interventions in "Iraq, Libya, Afghanistan, and Yugoslavia" were "really all handled within the framework of international law."[116] He further observed:

> This means that some can ignore everything, while we cannot protect the interests of the Russian-speaking and Russian population of Crimea. This will not happen. I would like everyone to understand this. We need to get rid of this temptation and attempts to arrange the world to one's liking, and to create a balanced system of interests and relations that has long been prescribed in the world, we only have to show some respect.[117]

Russian analysts point to Libya as evidence that the United States is acting in foreign interventions based on its whim. Furthermore, analysts describe Russian officials as feeling cheated because they did not view the agreed-upon UN Security Council Resolution 1973 as

---

[115] Specifically, Lavrov said,

> Some time ago they coined the term "humanitarian intervention" which basically means that if human rights are violated one can interfere, including with the use of military force. Then they invented the term "responsibility to protect" meaning that if a humanitarian crisis occurs somewhere for whatever reason—due to natural reasons or an armed conflict, the global community has the right to intervene. All these questions have been clearly answered in the UN General Assembly resolutions which say that interference is only allowed with the consent of the UN Security Council, i.e. the provision of the Charter has been confirmed. (Ministry of Foreign Affairs of the Russian Federation, "Foreign Minister Sergey Lavrov's Interview with Venezuelan State Television," October 2, 2015)

[116] Putin, 2014b.

[117] Putin, 2014b.

a mandate to use force to support the rebel forces in overthrowing Libyan leader Muammar Qaddafi.[118]

Overall, Russia sees U.S. intervention that is justified on the basis of gross violations of human rights as a growing threat to Russia's interests and as contradictory to its vision of the existing and desired international order. In line with the account of Russian views in the Chapter Two, Russian officials and analysts see Western foreign intervention as part of a coordinated vision of expanding the U.S.-led order. Most fundamentally, they fear that the United States could use similar justification to intervene in Russia's sphere of influence, undermining its exclusive control in this area.

In contrast with Western objectives of using foreign intervention to protect human rights, Russia's intervention in Syria that began in September 2015 appears motivated by very different objectives. Indeed, Russia's activities in Syria appear to be guided by several of Russia's underlying foreign policy interests—namely, its interest in great-power status and a desire to preserve noninterference in the domestic affairs of other countries—and by Russia's views of the current Western order as U.S. hegemony threatening its interests. At the 2015 Valdai meeting, Putin explained Russian intervention in Syria by highlighting Russia's goal of protecting the government of Syria as a means to stop terrorism,[119] as well as Russia's desire to be part of an international coalition to end conflict in the region.[120] Russian actions are thus

---

[118] Discussions with U.S. officials and analysts, Washington, D.C., March 2016; see also Christopher Chivvis, *Toppling Qaddafi: Libya and the Limits of Liberal Intervention*, New York: Cambridge University Press, 2014, pp. 60–61.

[119] Putin explained,

> After Syria's official authorities reached out to us for support, we made the decision to launch a Russian military operation in that nation. . . . The collapse of Syria's official authorities, for example, will only mobilise terrorists. Right now, instead of undermining them, we must revive them, strengthening state institutions in the conflict zone. (Vladimir Putin, "Meeting of the Valdai International Discussion Club," October 22, 2015a)

[120] Putin implicitly highlighted Russia's role in an international settlement over the U.S.-led political process:

> [I]sn't it time for the international community to coordinate all its actions with the people who live in these territories? I think that it's long overdue; these people—like

compatible with a perception that it is protecting the legitimate Assad regime from perceived U.S. support for moderate groups that seek to illegitimately unseat it. Further, Angela Stent directly connects Russia's engagement in Syria to its concerns about the U.S.-led security order, highlighting Russian objectives to "have a decisive say in who rules Syria, . . . recoup Russian influence in the Middle East, . . . [and] shift the focus from its role as an instigator of conflict [in Ukraine] to its new role in Syria as a responsible leader in the global campaign against terrorism."[121]

Critics of the Russian military intervention highlight Russian military strikes against civilian targets and note that Russia has not focused its attacks against the Islamic State of Iraq and Syria (ISIS)[122] but rather opponents of the Assad regime that the United States has

---

any people—should be treated with respect . . . . It is clear that Syria will need massive financial, economic and humanitarian assistance in order to heal the wounds of war. We need to determine the format within which we could do this work, getting donor nations and international financial institutions involved. . . . We are also close to starting an exchange of information with our western colleagues on militants' positions and movements. All these are certainly steps in the right direction. What's most important is to treat one another as allies in a common fight, to be honest and open. Only then can we guarantee victory over the terrorists. (Putin, 2015a)

[121] Angela Stent, "Putin's Power Play in Syria: How to Respond to Russia's Intervention," *Foreign Affairs*, January/February 2016. Matthew Dal Santo writes,

Western governments have long lamented the lack of transparency surrounding Putin's aims. But they're clear enough. The success of Putin's strategy in Syria will be measured in Moscow's success in asserting a right of consultation on issues of regional and global order where its interests are affected; not least in the Middle East where for almost 30 years the US has alone held sway. (Matthew Dal Santo, "Russia's Success in Syria Signals an Emerging Multipolar World Order," *Lowy Interpreter*, April 6, 2016)

See also Mark Mardell, "What Syria Reveals About the New World Order," BBC, October 3, 2016.

[122] The organization's name transliterates from Arabic as *al-Dawlah al-Islamiyah fi al-'Iraq wa al-Sham* (abbreviated as Da'ish or DAESH). In the West, it is commonly referred to as the Islamic State of Iraq and the Levant (ISIL), the Islamic State of Iraq and Syria, the Islamic State of Iraq and the Sham (both abbreviated as ISIS), or simply as the Islamic State (IS). Arguments abound as to which is the most accurate translation, but here we refer to the group as ISIS.

previously supported.[123] Although such actions may indeed undermine U.S. interests and activities in the region, they do not necessarily contradict Russia's declared strategy of support for the Assad government as a means of achieving its interests in the region and ensuring Russia's participation in any settlement.

Color Revolutions

Since the end of the Cold War, a series of pro-democracy and pro-Western protests have led to changes in government in the post-Soviet space; these have been referred to as *color revolutions*. While Western governments have a positive view of these events as the expression of free choice by the citizenry, Russian analysts and officials describe the events as Western-organized coups designed to subvert the legitimate authorities. As Trenin writes,

> Like NATO's enlargement, the color revolutions in Georgia (2003), Ukraine (2004), and Kyrgyzstan (2005) performed the task, in Western eyes, of expanding the space of freedom and democracy in the former Communist world. To the Kremlin, by contrast, the uprisings constituted a political challenge of regime change at home atop the geopolitical challenge of reducing Russia's influence beyond its border.[124]

The 2013–2014 Euromaidan revolution in Ukraine significantly increased the perception within Russia that the West was behind color revolutions and that such events could prose a threat to Russian national security. The Russian newspaper *Nezavisimaya Gazeta*, for example, quotes a Russian official explaining that "the legitimate political regime of Viktor Yanukovych was swept away through 'controlled' chaos. And it was replaced by a new regime that suits certain world powers." The article continues, "In Vladimir Putin's terms, there was a 'so-called color revolution, or, to call things by their names, simply

---

[123] Samantha Power, U.S. Ambassador to the UN, observed, "What Russia is sponsoring and doing is not counter-terrorism, it is barbarism" (Nichols and Bayoumy, 2016). See also Tom Perry and Jeff Mason, "Obama Urges Russia to Stop Bombing 'Moderate' Syria Rebels," Reuters, February 14, 2016.

[124] Trenin, 2014.

a coup d'etat provoked and financed from outside.'"[125] It is clear that the events of the Euromaidan revolution led to a significant change in Russian thinking and behavior, including the annexation of Crimea and support for separatism in eastern Ukraine. Some explanations for Russia's greater concern about the Euromaidan revolution compared with previous color revolutions include Russia's cultural and historical proximity to Ukraine, a concern over Russian forces based in Crimea, and a sense that the Euromaidan revolution was a clear demonstration that cooperation with the West was no longer possible.[126]

Following the events in Ukraine in 2014, Russian officials and analysts reframed Western activities as a military threat to Russia. Indeed, the 2015 Russian National Security Strategy included color revolutions supported by "foreign and international nongovernmental organizations" on a list of threats to Russia.[127] Russian military authors have also increasingly connected Ukraine to a larger set of Western

---

[125] Vladimir Mukhin, "Moscow Adjusts Military Doctrine: Events in Ukraine Are Making Russia Amend Documents Defining National Security Strategy," *Nezavisimaya Gazeta*, August 1, 2014. Similarly, Nikolai Patrushev, Secretary of Russian Security Council, noted, "The U.S. administration expects [its recent] anti-Russian measures to decrease quality of life for the population, give rise to mass protests and push Russian citizens to overthrow the current government using the scenario of the 'color revolutions'" (Paul Sonne, "U.S. Is Trying to Dismember Russia, Says Putin Adviser," *Wall Street Journal*, February 11, 2015).

[126] For example, Daniel Treisman writes that Russia's operation in Crimea is best understood as "an improvised gambit, developed under pressure, that was triggered by the fear of losing Russia's strategically important naval base in Sevastopol," although concerns about NATO enlargement are influential and there are voices within the Kremlin advocating for imperial expansion (Treisman, "Why Putin Took Crimea," *Foreign Affairs*, May/June 2016, p. 48). Furthermore, Lukin writes, "Moscow, having realised that it cannot establish friendly relations with Western countries without offering its complete political submission to them, has begun a real, not just rhetorical, political and economic turn to the non-Western world" (Lukin, 2016, p. 98). Author discussions with U.S., Ukrainian, and Russian analysts, March–April 2016, Washington, D.C., also contributed to this point.

[127] The strategy notes,

> The main threats to the state and public security are: . . . The activities of radical public associations and groups using nationalist and religious extremist ideology, foreign and international nongovernmental organizations, and financial and economic structures, and also individuals, focused on destroying the unity and territorial integrity of the Russian Federation, destabilizing the domestic political and social situation—including through inciting "color revolutions"—and destroying traditional Russian religious and moral values. (Russian Federation, 2015)

activities designed to systematically undermine legitimate governments. Gorenburg writes,

> Russian officials argue that military force is an integral part of all aspects of color revolutions. Western governments start by using non-military tactics to change opposing governments through color revolutions that utilize the protest potential of the population to engineer peaceful regime change. But military force is concealed behind this effort. If the protest potential turns out to be insufficient, military force is then used openly to ensure regime change.[128]

Hence, as with foreign intervention, Russian thinkers increasingly see color revolutions as a coordinated element of the U.S.-led order that will undermine Russian security interests, particularly in Russia's near abroad. From this point of view, the emphasis in the United States on free choice and the expansion of freedom and democracy, and the statement of an "open door" policy, offers a clear conflict with Russian interests in maintaining control and influence in its near abroad. Russian officials discount that Ukraine or other former Soviet republics would move away from Russia without Western influence—and, in any case, oppose their right to do so. Russia therefore seeks to develop the capabilities to resist future Western-led color revolutions that might further undermine Russian security.[129]

---

[128] Dmitry Gorenburg, *Countering Color Revolutions: Russia's New Security Strategy and Its Implications for U.S. Policy*, PONARS Eurasia, Memo 342, September 2014.

[129] See Robert Coalson's translation of a 2013 article by Chief of the General Staff Valeriy Gerasimov (Robert Coalson, "Top Russian General Lays Bare Putin's Plan for Ukraine," *Huffington Post*, November 2, 2014; Valeriy Gerasimov, "Tsennost' Nauki v Predvidenii [The Value of Science in Foresight]," *Voenno-Promyshlennyj Kuryer* [Military-Industrial Courier], February 27, 2013).

Information Security

Russian views of the concept of "information security" are fundamentally different from Western ones. Western discussions about this topic are often considered in the context of cybersecurity or criminal activities and are based on a presumption of the value of the free flow of information. By contrast, Russia (following, to some extent, the Soviet legacy) has sought to gain exclusive control over information distributed within its own borders. Indeed, control of information is a priority for the Putin government, shown by the emphasis it has placed on controlling Russian media and domestic information since it came to power in 2000.[130] Based on these views, Russia, with China, has pursued new international norms about information security.

Russia's ideas about information control are formalized in its Information Security Doctrine, which notes,

> Russia will take necessary measures to ensure national and international information security, prevent political, economic and social threats to the state's security that emerge in information space in order to combat terrorism and other criminal threats in the area of application of information and communication technologies, [and] prevent them from being used for military and political purposes that run counter to international law, *including actions aimed at interference in the internal affairs and constituting a threat to international peace, security and stability.*[131]

This language shows Russia's concern about foreign involvement in its domestic information space—meaning the totality of the information, ideas, and communication or transfer of information within

---

[130] See Putin's strategy for governing Russia published in "The Reform of the Administration of the President of the Russian Federation," trans. Petr Podkopaev, Karen Dawisha, and James Nealy, *Kommersant*, May 5, 2000; and Karen Dawisha, *Putin's Kleptocracy: Who Owns Russia?* New York: Simon & Schuster, 2014.

[131] Ministry of Foreign Affairs of the Russian Federation, *The Information Security Doctrine of the Russian Federation*, December 29, 2008, emphasis added.

a society[132]—as an essential security interest.[133] In contrast, the U.S. Constitution explicitly limits a U.S. government role in the control of domestic information, and the free flow of information is a priority for Western governments.[134] To some extent, Russian officials appear concerned about abstract and diffuse problems, such as the "depreciation of spiritual values," but they also clearly worry that foreign-funded organizations will influence the population in ways that would threaten the regime.

Russian support for an international convention on "information security" shows both its belief in its rightful ability to control information within its borders and its desire to develop the international order to reflect its views. Russia's proposed convention draws from similar language in its Information Security Doctrine. For example, the proposal notes a threat of the "manipulation of the flow of information in the information space of other governments, disinformation or the concealment of information with the goal of adversely affecting the psychological or spiritual state of society, or eroding traditional cul-

---

[132] Dmitry Adamsky writes,

> Current Russian doctrines and policy perceive cyber space as an integral part of the broader information space. Russian official terminology differentiates between: *informational space*—all spheres where societal perception takes shape; *information*—content shaping perception and decision-making; and *informational infrastructure*—technological media that gives digital and analog expression to the first two, essentially cognitive-perceptional, components. (Dmitry Adamsky, *Cross-Domain Coercion: The Current Russian Art of Strategy*, Institut Français des Relations Internationales Security Studies Center, Proliferation Papers No. 54, November 2015, p. 28)

[133] Russia's Information Security Doctrine explains that the information sphere

> represents an assemblage of information, information infrastructure, entities engaged in the collection, formation, dissemination and use of information, and a system governing public relations arising out of these conditions. The information sphere as a system-forming factor of societal life actively influences the state of the political, economic, defense, and other components of Russian Federation security. (Ministry of Foreign Affairs of the Russian Federation, 2008)

[134] See, for example, U.S. Department of State, "Joint Press Statement for the 2015 U.S.-European Union Information Society Dialogue," Washington, D.C., April 2015.

tural, moral, ethical, and aesthetic values."[135] The convention suggests principles that would enhance Russia's ability to control information, including that "each State Party in the information space must . . . conform to the universally recognized principles and norms of international law, including . . . noninterference into the internal affairs of other States."[136] Russia's position on information security reflects a longstanding conflict over the free flow of information: During the Cold War, Western countries sought to maintain the ability to broadcast into Soviet territory, while the Soviet Union sought to block or stop Western broadcasts.[137]

Russia has also used the information security convention, among other cooperation with China on cyber and information issues, as an attempt to develop its relationship with China. Russian reporting on the convention highlights Russia's growing cooperation with China and the two countries' shared interests in developing the convention to address the critical challenges of information security.[138] Western countries have responded to the UN process by reinterpreting the Russian proposal to focus on cybersecurity, which is clearly a shared concern.[139] However, cooperation between Russia and the West on cyber and information security will ultimately be very difficult given the fundamentally different goals in this area.

---

[135] Ministry of Foreign Affairs of the Russian Federation, *Convention on International Information Security*, September 22, 2011.

[136] Ministry of Foreign Affairs of the Russian Federation, 2011.

[137] See A. Ross Johnson, "History," Radio Free Europe/Radio Liberty, December 2008.

[138] Alexandra Kulikova, "China-Russia Cyber-Security Pact: Should the US Be Concerned?" *Russia Direct*, May 21, 2015.

[139] UK Foreign and Commonwealth Office, "Response to General Assembly Resolution 69/28: 'Developments in the Field of Information and Telecommunications in the Context of International Security,'" May 2015.

Conclusion

Russian leaders articulate a view that the overall logic of the current international order is U.S. hegemony, justified through claims of spreading liberal democracy. Despite this negative view of the current overall order, Russia has a range of views on the various components of order. When a given component of order does not threaten Russia's security or position in its near abroad, it seeks to build cooperation, as evidenced in Russian support for the UN, the development of international economic institutions, and other areas. However, there are several components of order for which the U.S. approach conflicts with Russia's interests in its region; such components include the enlargement of NATO and the EU and Western of norms of sovereignty, democracy, and human rights. These are key areas of direct conflict between the United States and Russia—and areas in which Russia will likely continue to take action to undermine the U.S.-led order.

CHAPTER FOUR

Alternative Russian Views

The previous chapters have examined the official Russian political leadership's position on the international order, with a particular focus on the attitudes of President Putin, who is believed to exercise considerable control over Russia's foreign policy.[1] We have also highlighted the views of think tanks and analysts who adopt a position fairly close to that of the regime. This chapter analyzes alternative views within Russia.

Russian Military Views

A review of the Russian military literature published in military newspapers and journals over the past ten years reveals that the military community has virtually no variance from the government perspective on the international order.

Russian military writings offered a clear description of how the U.S. pursuit of a unipolar world posed a threat to Russia before Russian senior leaders made a similar argument. In 2003, one year before becoming the chief of the Russian General Staff, General Yuri Baluyevsky noted, "The world can only be multipolar, otherwise it would be unstable. . . . [T]he willingness to ignore the opinion of other countries and to openly refuse to yield to anything not in one's interests

---

[1] Dmitri Trenin, *Russia's Breakout from the Post–Cold War System: The Drivers of Putin's Course*, Moscow: Carnegie Moscow Center, December 2014, p. 7; Hill and Gaddy, 2013.

does not consolidate moral authority."[2] A 2006 article from a Russian military journal observed, "it would be, mildly speaking, shortsighted (and self-destructive) for Russia to pursue a policy that would ignore the fact that the USA and its closest allies are striving for the unipolar world and are looking forward to NATO's enlargement to the East."[3] In 2010, an article analyzing the more-recent combat actions of the United States stated, "The armed conflicts of the late 20th and early 21st centuries have been a graphic demonstration of the United States' desire for a unipolar world and its determination to solve any problems by force, ignoring the opinion of the world community."[4] Recently, Chief of the General Staff Gerasimov and others have highlighted the threat of the Arab Spring and the U.S.-backed color revolutions in the former Soviet Union.[5] Hence, there appears to be a strong consensus within the Russian military establishment: The United States, in seeking to establish an international order led by a sole power, threatens Russia's national security interests.

Russian Opposition Views

While there is certainly broad agreement across varying strata of the Russian foreign policy establishment on the issue of international order, there is a small enclave of opposition figures, mostly within Moscow,

---

[2]   Yuri Baluyevsky, "Strategicheskaya Stabilnost' v Epokhu Globalizatsii [Strategic Stability in an Era of Globalization]," trans. Clinton Reach, *Rossiya v Globalnoj Politike [Russia in Global Affairs]*, No. 4, November 28, 2003.

[3]   A. A. Paderin, "Policy and Military Strategy: A Unity Lesson," *Military Thought*, April 1, 2006–June 30, 2006, p. 23. A 2009 essay from *Military Thought* similarly argued, "As previously, the Americans will continue actively to foist their values on the rest of the world relying on all the force and assets available to them" (A. Yu Maruyev, "Russia and the U.S.A. in Confrontation: Military and Political Aspects," *Military Thought*, July 1, 2009–September 30, 2009, p. 3).

[4]   S. L. Tashlykov, "General and Particular Features of Present-Day Conflicts Involving the U.S. and Its Allies," *Military Thought*, July 1, 2010–September 30, 2010.

[5]   Valeriy Gerasimov, "Po Opytu Sirii [According to the Experience of Syria]," *Voennoe Promyshlennoe Kuryer [Military Industrial Courier]*, March 9, 2016.

who have a different perception of Russia's role in the world. In brief, this opposition view is based on the idea that Russia should promote democracy at home and abroad and work to integrate itself into the Western world instead of trying to balance against it.

Yabloko, a leading opposition party, has come out strongly against the Russian intervention in Syria, arguing that Russia "initiated a one-sided interference into the Syrian armed conflict" that was characterized by "anti-Americanism [and] anti-European and self-isolating foreign policy." Yabloko's statement went on to assert that Russian policy in Syria sought to solidify a "sustainably antidemocratic model within the country" and was accompanied by "propaganda that firmly identifies patriotism with chauvinistic veneration of the authorities."[6]

The platform of Parnas, an opposition party headed by Mikhail Kasyanov, the prime minister of Russia from 2000 to 2004, argues that Russia's current foreign policy is carried out by a leadership that is "actively exploiting post-imperial and post-Soviet complexes for the mobilization of the population on the basis of confrontation with the West."[7] The conduct of Russian foreign policy over the past few years, according to Parnas, has "isolated the country from the civilized world (exit from the G-8, sanctions, the conflict with the European Council and other international organizations)" and returned Russian society to a state in which there is a feeling that "large-scale war with the West is a real possibility."[8]

Other individual opposition leaders within Russia lament the direction that Russian foreign policy has taken under Putin and do not express the same assuredness that the current U.S.-led international order is broken. Echoing back to positions advocated by Foreign Minister Kozyrev early in the post–Cold War period, some even support closer political and economic integration with the West as opposed to confrontation or counter-balancing. Dmitry Gudkov, a deputy

[6] Yabloko Political Committee, "Operation in Syria and the Threats to the National Security," Moscow: Russian Democratic Party Yabloko, November 16, 2015.

[7] People's Freedom Party/Parnas, "Platforma Domkraticheskoy Koalitsii Parnas [Platform of the Democratic Coalition of Parnas]," Moscow, July 5, 2015.

[8] People's Freedom Party/Parnas, 2015.

in the State Duma and an opposition figure, stated that "escapades in Ukraine" had significantly damaged the country and that Russia "needs to reconcile with the West and attract investment" because confrontation has had significant negative consequences.[9]

While opposition parties in Russia promote a drastically different vision of Russia's foreign policy and its place in the world, the parties do not enjoy much support from the Russian population in general. Neither Yabloko nor Parnas currently holds a seat in the Russian parliament. In the 2011 Duma elections, Yabloko received a mere 3.43 percent of the total vote.[10] After United Russia, which is the ruling party in the Russian government, the second-most popular party in Russia is the Communist Party. As has been the case for hundreds of years in Russia, "Westernizers" have struggled to make inroads with a majority of the Russian people,[11] and they are handicapped by the current government's control over much of the Russian mass media.

Eurasianism and Radical Views

The regime's views are far from the most radical views of Russia's place within the current international system. Perhaps the most visible and coherent of the more radical and aggressive views is Eurasianism. Eurasianism traces its roots to the days of the Soviet émigrés of the 1920s and, more recently, to Lev Gumilev, who expanded Eurasianist ideas throughout the latter half of the Soviet period. Since the collapse of the Soviet Union, the most-visible proponents of Eurasianist ideas are Russian intellectuals Aleksandr Dugin and Aleksandr Panarin, each of whom argued for a version of reintegration of the post-Soviet space into a "Eurasian" sphere of influence for Russia. The Eurasianists are some-

---

[9] Dmitri Gudkov, "Osoboe Mnenie [Unique Perspective]," trans. Clinton Reach, *Echo of Moscow*, November 19, 2015.

[10] Centre for the Study of Public Policy at the University of Strathclyde, "Final Result of the Duma Election, 4 December 2011," Moscow: The Levada Center, August 12, 2015.

[11] See Richard Pipes, *Russian Conservatism and Its Critics*, New Haven, Conn.: Yale University Press, June 28, 2007.

times cited as influential in the development of Russia's military and foreign policy discourse, including the development of Russia's activity in Ukraine,[12] but they do not appear to directly influence governance.

Dugin, perhaps the most prominent Eurasianist in Russia today, offers some concepts that appear to be in sync with and perhaps influential to Russian leadership. For example, Dugin wrote about creating a Eurasian Union as far back as 2001, when he penned his Eurasist Manifesto as a platform for a Eurasia political party. In the document, Dugin writes, "In the sphere of foreign policy, Eurasism [now called Eurasianism] implies a wide process of strategic integration. Reconstruction on the basis of the CIS of a solid Eurasian Union (analogue to the USSR on a new ideological, economic and administrative basis)."[13] Dugin's proposed Eurasian Union is very different from the Eurasian Economic Union that was eventually created. Nevertheless, there remains some common ground. For example, in his article in *Izvestia*, Putin observes that the goal of the Eurasian Union is to create "a powerful supranational association capable of becoming one of the poles in the modern world and serving as an efficient bridge between Europe and the dynamic Asia-Pacific region."[14] Two years after Putin's article, Dugin reaffirmed his support for the Eurasian Union: "[T]he world must have several poles and . . . among these poles the Eurasian one should take its place: the American, European and Far East poles."[15] Like Putin and Medvedev, Dugin has also condemned the unipolar world and argued for the "principle of multi-polarity, standing against the unipolar globalism imposed by the atlantists [the West]."[16]

---

[12] See U.S. Army Special Operations Command, *"Little Green Men": A Primer on Modern Russian Unconventional Warfare, Ukraine 2013–2014*, Fort Bragg, N.C., undated, pp. 15–17; and Jolanta Darczewska, *The Anatomy of Russian Information Warfare: The Crimean Operation—A Case Study*, Warsaw: Centre for Eastern Studies (OSW), May 2014.

[13] Aleksandr Dugin, "Eurasia Above All: Manifesto of the Eurasist Movement," trans. M. Conserva, *Arctogaia*, January 1, 2001.

[14] Putin, 2011.

[15] Aleksandr Dugin, "Eurasian Keys to the Future," *The Fourth Political Theory*, May 2012.

[16] Aleksandr Dugin, "The Eurasist Vision: Basic Principles of the Eurasist Doctrinal Platform," *The Fourth Political Theory*, undated.

Looking more closely at Dugin's thought, although there is some overlap between his ideas and the more-mainstream Russian views discussed in Chapter Three, there are also significant divergences. Dugin's central geopolitical thesis is that, because of its unique Asian history and geography, Russia is fundamentally incompatible with the West. Instead, Dugin argues, Russia should seek to dominate the Eurasian space, which he defined as all of the republics of the former Soviet Union and certain elements of other neighboring countries. Within that space, Russia should create an environment that promotes "authoritarianism, hierarchy, and the posing of community-based, nation-state principles against small human, individualist, hedonistic, and economic interests."[17] Under his schema, Dugin further advocates that Central and Western Europe should fall into an area of German dominance, free from the corrupting influence of the "atlanticist" countries of Great Britain and the United States.[18] John Dunlop draws from Dugin's writings to note preferred domains for different countries: Estonia should be within Germany's sphere, while Poland, Latvia, and Lithuania should have "special status" within the Russian-controlled Eurasian sphere.[19] Like many other Russians, Dugin discounts Ukraine's validity as a real country: "Ukraine as a state has no geopolitical meaning. It has no particular cultural import or universal

---

[17] Aleksandr Dugin, "The Great War of Continents," in *Konspirologiya* [*Conspirology*], Moscow: Arctogaya, 1993.

[18] John B. Dunlop, "Aleksandr Dugin's *Foundations of Geopolitics*," *Demokratizatsiya*, Vol. 12, No. 1, January 31, 2004.

[19] Dunlop summarizes Dugin's views on the Balkans from Dugin's 1997 *Foundations of Geopolitics*:

> Dugin assigns "the north of the Balkan peninsula from Serbia to Bulgaria" to what he terms the "Russian South" (p. 343). "Serbia is Russia," a subheading in the book declares unambiguously (p. 462). In Dugin's opinion, all of the states of the "Orthodox collectivist East" with time will seek to establish binding ties to "Moscow the Third Rome," thus rejecting the snares of the "rational-individualistic West" (pp. 389, 393). The states of Romania, Macedonia, "Serbian Bosnia," and even NATO-member Greece in time, Dugin predicts, will become constituent parts of the Eurasian-Russian Empire (pp. 346, 383). (Dunlop, 2004)

significance, no geographic uniqueness, no ethnic exclusiveness."[20] In addition, China poses a threat to Russia, so Dugin recommends seeking assistance from Korea, Vietnam, India, and Japan to ensure the "territorial disintegration, splintering and the political and administrative partition of the [Chinese] state."[21] With the possible exception of Ukraine, these do not appear to be realistic concepts that have any significant buy-in from Russian officials.

Furthermore, while Dugin is reported to have connections and ties with Russian officials, including the Russian military leadership,[22] and although Russian leaders may cite his work or ideas, it does not appear that he is directly influential in Russian policymaking. He is perhaps best thought of as an extremist provocateur with some limited and peripheral impact than as an influential analyst with a direct impact on policy. He does not appear to have direct involvement with the major political parties—such as United Russia, the Communist Party, the Liberal Democratic Party of Russia, and Rodina—advocating anti-Western and aggressive regional policies.[23] He was also removed from his position at Moscow State University after calling for the killing of Ukrainian nationalists, and he has offered significant criticism of Putin's policies in Ukraine.[24]

Dugin is not the only Eurasianist calling for a more aggressive Russian foreign policy based on more-radical views of international order. Igor Panarin, the dean of the academy for Russia's Foreign Min-

---

[20] Quoted in Dunlop, 2004.

[21] Quoted in Dunlop, 2004.

[22] For example, in a 2014 article, former Chief of the General Staff Yuri Baluyevsky attributes Dugin with identifying the Western-influenced "fifth column" opposition that is attempting to undermine Russia (Yuri Baluyevsky and Musa Khamzatov "Globalizatsiya i Voennoe Delo [Globalization and Military Affairs]," trans. Clinton Reach, *Nezavisimoe Voennoe Obozreniye [Independent Military Review]*, August 8, 2014). See also Dmitri Trenin, *The End of Eurasia: Russia on the Border Between Geopolitics and Globalization*, Washington, D.C.: Carnegie Endowment for International Peace, 2001, p. 33.

[23] Marlène Laruelle, *Russian Eurasianism: Ideology of Empire*, Washington, D.C.: Woodrow Wilson Center Press, 2012, p. 113.

[24] See Catherine Fitzpatrick, "Russia This Week: Dugin Dismissed from Moscow State University?" *Interpreter Magazine*, June 24, 2014; see also Laruelle, 2012.

istry, sees an elaborate and multifaceted "information war" against Russia by the West, and, according to one account, he urges the creation of "a new union of states, extending from Egypt to China, as a counterbalance to this falling empire. The Eurasian Ruthenia would be at the core of this union of states."[25] But Marlène Laruelle, a U.S. scholar who has written extensively about Eurasianism, has argued that one should not overestimate the influence of Eurasianism on contemporary Russian foreign policy. She writes, "Neither Yeltsin nor Putin has ever made Eurasianist statements in the sense of using a culturalist terminology to argue that Russia has an Asian *essence*."[26] Nevertheless, Eurasianist and other more-radical imperial ideas remain options for Russian policymakers to draw from as they develop foreign policy.

Conclusion

There is a significant consensus of views within Russia that is shared not only by the regime and mainstream think tanks but also by the Russian military. There are, of course, nuances in views about particular issues, but many Russian officials and analysts share the view that the U.S.-led order is increasingly threatening Russian interests in its near abroad. There are members of the opposition in Russia who advocate policies that are more pro-Western, but these individuals appear few in number and not particularly influential. There are also more-extreme views in the other direction—notably, the Eurasianist perspectives of Dugin and Panarin. But even though mainstream analysts and the regime do reference Eurasianist ideas and thinkers, these theorists do not seem especially influential.

Indeed, accounts of Russian foreign policy indicate that the Putin administration's decisionmaking structures are highly centralized under the President, so the influence of alternative views may be

---

[25] Darczewska, 2014, p. 17.

[26] Laruelle, 2012, p. 8.

minimal in any case.[27] Although the administration has deliberative structures that, in theory, integrate the positions of lower-level officials, such as the Russian National Security Council, analysts emphasize that most decisions are made by Putin, informed through informal discussions with a very small number of advisers.[28] Putin's decisions are likely informed by a range of considerations, one of which may be the domestic popularity of his policies. Still, so long as Putin retains his control of the Russian government—and there does not appear to be any clear competitor—the direct influence of opposition views into Russian foreign policy will likely be limited. The foreign policy perspective of the regime will continue to evolve over time, and it may be that more-liberal or nationalist thinkers could inform the regime to adopt a more aggressive or conciliatory strategy. Based on the analysis in this report, however, there is no indication that the basic Russian thinking about the logic of the international order or its components will change significantly in the near future.

---

[27] Hill and Gaddy write, "Everybody knowing what they have to do and when they have to do it—as well as knowing that they will be accountable to the man at the top—is the idealized essence of Putin's system" (Hill and Gaddy, 2013, p. 209).

[28] Author discussions with analysts, Cambridge, UK, and Washington, D.C., February–April 2016. Fiona Hill writes,

> [Putin] may listen to the counsel of his friends or not. We do not actually know. The circle is extremely narrow and difficult to penetrate, even for supposed Russian political insiders. What we do know is that there is no oligarchy or separate set of economic, business, or political interests that compete with Putin. In the end, he makes the decisions. (Fiona Hill, "Putin: The One-Man Show the West Doesn't Understand," *Bulletin of the Atomic Scientists*, Vol. 72, No. 3, 2016, p. 140)

CHAPTER FIVE

Conclusion and Policy Implications

There is a consensus view within Russian foreign policy discussions that the underlying logic of the current international order—U.S. hegemony—poses a fundamental threat to Russian interests. Russia seeks to protect the security of the regime, its influence within its region, and its influence as a great power, and it sees U.S. leadership, and its continuing effort to expand liberal democracy, as a threat to these goals. Until around 2007, Russian officials appear to have believed that integrating Russia into the Western order could achieve these goals, in part because the West would accommodate Russia's core interests. Although Russia has not abandoned the possibility of cooperation with the West on some issues, a range of events—such as growing Russian wealth, NATO and EU enlargement, and frustration with WTO accession—have led Russia to abandon closer participation in the U.S.-led order in favor of building new institutions that it controls and working to undermine the Western order. From a Russian point of view, Western policies are out of proportion with the balance of power, dangerous to peace and stability, and contrary to established rules or norms of international relations.

Western officials tend to argue that Russia misjudges the threat from the West, explain that there is no plan to undermine Russian interests at home or in the near abroad, and claim that the countries in the near abroad are exercising their own free will. The reality of Western intentions, however, does not change Russian views or the uncertainty about Western intentions. Just as the West partly designs its policy on the basis of uncertainty about Russia's intentions, it is not surprising that Russia's foreign policy is partly premised on uncertainty about the West.[1]

This is not to say that Russian beliefs should determine U.S. policy. However, Russia's views do suggest policy options. By isolating Russian views of the components of order outlined in Chapter Three, it becomes clear that Russian and U.S. interests are not always opposed; the maintenance of the UN system is one example of a shared interest. By recognizing that Russian views of the current international order vary based on the effects on core Russian interests, it becomes possible to identify points of cooperation and contestation. Where there are shared interests, it may be possible to pursue cooperation.

With regard to points of contestation, there are no easy answers about how to resolve the conflict between Russia's concerns and U.S. interests in the current framing of the European political and security order. The desired U.S. approach to Russia with respect to order critically depends on two concepts: (1) the importance of enabling former Soviet republics to freely join Western institutions and (2) whether Russia will limit its aggression in Europe if its interests are recognized. There are differing beliefs about both concepts. With regard to the first concept, some see Russia's desire for influence beyond its borders as legitimate, while others place a priority on deepening and expanding the EU and NATO. With regard to the second concept, some believe that Russia would take any Western assurance as a sign of weakness, while others believe that Russia may be assuaged by words or actions that downplay or limit EU and NATO enlargement.

With these underlying concepts in mind, and drawing from the analysis in this report, we highlight three major areas of contestation that have the potential to undermine Russia's relationship with the United States and the U.S.-led order, and we sketch the broad options for U.S. policy in these areas. While we do not recommend a specific approach, we highlight how the Russian views of order constrain U.S. policy options.

---

[1]   See John J. Mearsheimer, *The Tragedy of Great Power Politics*, New York: W. W. Norton, 2001, p. 31; and David Shlapak and Michael Johnson, *Reinforcing Deterrence on NATO's Eastern Flank: Wargaming the Defense of the Baltics*, Santa Monica, Calif.: RAND Corporation, RR-1253-A, 2016, p. 3.

The Open Door and Russia's Sphere of Influence

The most fundamental point of contestation between the United States and Russia on the international order is the status of Belarus, Georgia, Moldova, and Ukraine—all former Soviet republics. While Russia views these countries as part of its exclusive sphere of influence (based on its status as a sovereign great power), the United States views these as free, sovereign countries that have the right to join Western institutions and eschew Russian influence.

While this issue has long troubled relations between Russia and Western countries, the effort by Ukraine to sign the Association Agreement and its Deep and Comprehensive Free Trade Area agreement with the EU brought this issue to a head. Ukraine also offers a clear demonstration of the dilemma, which applies equally to Belarus, Georgia, Moldova, and other countries. As it stands, the United States officially recognizes the right of Ukraine to pursue EU and NATO membership and, at the same time, informally downplays Ukraine's future accession. The United States has also offered military and economic support to Ukraine, though carefully limiting and calibrating this support (e.g., no lethal aid) because of concerns about a backlash from Russia. In both cases, the United States is in the difficult situation of wanting to help Ukraine while being unwilling to commit to its defense. Without a clear perspective that Ukraine may join NATO, and given the limits of U.S. support, Ukrainian leaders may become doubtful about the extent of Western support and about Ukraine's future in the West. The Western agenda of integration is thus undermined by the ambiguity about the West's commitment to the country.[2]

To address this dilemma, the United States has two basic options, though neither is likely to be fully implemented on its own. First, the United States can compromise on the existing concepts of the liberal order by limiting NATO and EU enlargement. Current efforts to informally downplay the membership prospects of Ukraine and Georgia may seem to limit the potential for enlargement, but these efforts are

---

[2] Author discussions with U.S., European, and Ukrainian officials and policy analysts, Washington, D.C., 2016. See also Samuel Charap and Jeremy Shapiro, "US-Russian Relations: The Middle Cannot Hold," *Bulletin of the Atomic Scientist*, Vol. 72, No. 3, April 14, 2016, pp. 151–152.

contradicted by public statements of the continued open-door policy, as well as by continued assistance to Ukraine. A more consistent strategy of limiting EU or NATO integration would require public statements rejecting the further accession of the former Soviet republics. Along these lines, Samuel Charap and Jeremy Shaprio recommend clarifying that "the policy of Euro-Atlantic institutional enlargement in post-communist Europe, despite its past successes, has run its course," and they instead recommend "new institutional arrangements for the 'in-between' states" that would recognize Russian interests.[3]

This strategy would recognize Russian interests and could fundamentally change Russia's views of the international order and its resultant foreign policy. In particular, it could improve Russia's cooperation on areas of shared interest, such as combating terrorism, reducing conflict in the Middle East, and limiting North Korea's nuclear capabilities.[4] There are, however, significant risks and challenges to compromising on the objectives of the liberal order. Most fundamentally, there is no guarantee that Russia will reciprocate with greater cooperation. The views of order presented in this report highlight the limits of Russia's interests, but those interests could change. Russia may interpret any U.S. declaration limiting its intentions in eastern Europe as a sign of weakness. Although Russia's perceptions of its own sphere of influence may not currently include NATO countries, it may adopt more-aggressive imperial rhetoric that would threaten the Baltic states or other NATO members. Leaving Ukraine and the other former Soviet republics outside of NATO may make other U.S. partners question U.S. commitment to their security. The compromise of liberal objectives and the negotiation of a specific agreement with Russia would also be extremely challenging from the perspective of U.S. domestic politics. It would officially reduce U.S. commitment to the security and integration of the former Soviet republics and bring back echoes

---

[3]   Charap and Shapiro, 2016, p. 153.

[4]   Indeed, Charap and Shapiro identify the goal as "achieving stability in US-Russian relations, based on an understanding that this relationship needs to function in order for Washington to effectively pursue its objectives globally" (Charap and Shapiro, 2016, p. 152).

of Yalta, where Franklin D. Roosevelt and Joseph Stalin decided the future of eastern Europe without the input of the respective countries.

A second strategy to address the dilemma would be to effectively double down on the current European security order, maintain or strengthen efforts to integrate the former Soviet countries, and use a wide range of military and political tools to deter Russian aggression both toward the EU and NATO and toward countries in Russia's neighborhood. In March 2015 testimony to the U.S. Senate Committee on Foreign Relations, American foreign policy expert Ian Brezinski urged "supporting Ukraine's Euro-Atlantic integration," including by "for example us[ing] [NATO's] Warsaw meeting in July to reiterate its vision that Ukraine and Georgia 'will become members of NATO.'"[5] The advantage of such a policy is that it would reinforce U.S. objectives of building a larger and deeper democratic order, demonstrating the rights of Ukraine and other former Soviet republics to secure their own future. However, as outlined earlier, it would also mean continuing to pursue a view of order that Russia finds threatening to its basic security interests. Russia would still be able and motivated to use the tools at its disposal to undermine U.S. policy and harm the U.S.-led order. Based on the increasingly harsh view within Russia about U.S. intentions, an effort by the United States to double down on the current European order could diminish the potential for cooperation on other issues for which the United States and Russia share interests.

Within the constraints of U.S. and European politics, probably neither a pure strategy of limiting enlargement or one of doubling down is feasible; therefore, U.S. policy toward the European political and security order will likely involve some elements of both.

---

[5] Ian Brezinski, *Ukrainian Reforms Two Years After the Maidan Revolution and the Russian Invasion*, Testimony Before the Senate Committee on Foreign Relations, Washington, D.C.: Government Printing Office, March 15, 2016, pp. 6–7.

Democracy Promotion

A second area of contestation is U.S. policy toward democracy promotion. The U.S. view of the international order, as outlined in national strategy documents, sees democracy promotion as beneficial for both normative and practical reasons.[6] While the United States does not explicitly call for regime change in Russia or its near abroad, and indeed takes pains to avoid such rhetoric, Russian officials clearly see the potential for such a policy through U.S. support for color revolutions, support for pro-democracy groups, and desire for the free flow of information. Given the discussion of Russian beliefs in this report, it is difficult to imagine public or private statements that would convince Russian officials and analysts to reject the possibility of U.S. aggressive intentions. At the same time, explicitly abandoning support for democracy and freedom of choice is likely inconsistent with the values underlying U.S. foreign policy for the past several decades.

Intervention and Sovereignty

A third area of contestation between Russia and the United States is their differing views on sovereignty and foreign intervention. Russia emphasizes the norm of noninterference and, at the same time, demands exclusive authority to intervene in its own region. By contrast, the United States has emphasized that sovereignty is conditional on preventing mass atrocity and has used military action, without a UN mandate, in countries where atrocities or gross violations of human rights were occurring. Russia's ongoing intervention in Syria also could lead to clashes because Russia's objectives of supporting the Assad regime directly conflict with U.S. support to moderate rebel groups. Furthermore, although both the United States and Russia claim to seek to destroy ISIS, there may be little practical means of collaborating given the disparate objectives of both countries.[7] There has also been

---

[6]   Mazarr et al., 2016, p. 47–51.

[7]   See, for example, Christopher Chivvis, "Time to Bury Plans for Counter-Terrorism Cooperation with Russia in Syria," *National Interest*, September 23, 2016.

disagreement and friction from U.S.-led interventions in Libya, Iraq, and the Balkans. These interventions indicate, from a Russian perspective, that the United States might take aggressive action in Russia's near abroad or another region without Russia's permission. The idea of a U.S.-led intervention into a former Soviet country may seem implausible, but Russian discourse takes the possibility seriously and connects Western intervention in other regions with potential intervention in Russia's desired sphere of influence. Hence, the United States will not foreswear the possibility of another intervention without a UN mandate, and Russia cannot condone the United States acting outside the UN system. Doing so would undermine Russia's fundamental interests in being a great power.

The United States and Russia share some objectives, including avoiding major war, improving economic cooperation, and combating terrorism. But officials on both sides are concerned about the risk of escalation in Syria, the Baltics, and Ukraine. While there is theoretical room for negotiation, both sides remain committed to incompatible views of the international order. Until there is room for at least temporary compromise on these underlying objectives, there appears limited potential for improving the adversarial relationship between the United States and Russia.

References

Adamsky, Dmitry, *Cross-Domain Coercion: The Current Russian Art of Strategy*, Institut Français des Relations Internationales Security Studies Center, Proliferation Papers No. 54, November 2015. As of January 23, 2017: http://www.ifri.org/sites/default/files/atoms/files/pp54adamsky.pdf

Aleksashenko, Sergey, "For Ukraine, Moldova, and Georgia Free Trade with Europe and Russia Is Possible," Beirut, Lebanon: Carnegie Middle East Center, July 3, 2014. As of January 23, 2017: http://carnegie-mec.org/2014/07/03/ for-ukraine-moldova-and-georgia-free-trade-with-europe-and-russia-is-possible

Allison, Roy, "Russian 'Deniable' Intervention in Ukraine: How and Why Russia Broke the Rules," *International Affairs*, Vol. 90, No. 6, November 2014, pp. 1269–1275.

Amos, Howard, "Russia Welcomes Syria Ceasefire as Proof of Great Power Status," *International Business Times*, February 29, 2016. As of January 23, 2017: http://www.ibtimes.com/ russia-welcomes-syria-ceasefire-proof-great-power-status-2327032

Antonenko, Oksana, "Russia, NATO and European Security After Kosovo," *Survival: Global Politics and Strategy*, Vol. 41, No. 4, Winter 1999, pp. 124–144.

Arbatova, Nadezhda K., and Alexander A. Dynkin, "World Order After Ukraine," *Survival: Global Politics and Strategy*, Vol. 58, No. 1, February–March 2016, pp. 71–90.

Åslund, Anders, "Russia's Accession to the World Trade Organization," *Eurasian Geography and Economics*, Vol. 48, No. 3, 2007, pp. 289–305.

———, "Why Doesn't Russia Join the WTO?" *Washington Quarterly*, Vol. 33, No. 2, April 2010, pp. 49–63.

Asmus, Ronald D., *Opening NATO's Door*, New York: Columbia University Press, 2002.

Baluyevsky, Yuri, "Strategicheskaya Stabilnost' v Epokhu Globalizatsii [Strategic Stability in an Era of Globalization]," trans. Clinton Reach, *Rossiya v Globalnoj Politike [Russia in Global Affairs]*, No. 4, November 28, 2003. As of January 23, 2017:
http://www.globalaffairs.ru/number/n_2114

Baluyevsky, Yuri, and Musa Khamzatov, "Globalizatsiya i Voennoe Delo [Globalization and Military Affairs]," trans. Clinton Reach, *Nezavisimoe Voennoe Obozreniye [Independent Military Review]*, August 8, 2014.

Barabanov, Oleg, Timofey Bordachev, Fyodor Lukyanov, Andrey Sushentsov, Dmitry Suslov, and Ivan Timofeev, *War and Peace in the 21st Century: International Stability and Balance of the New Type*, Moscow: Valdai International Discussion Club, January 21, 2016. As of January 23, 2017:
http://valdaiclub.com/files/9635/

Barbashin, Anton, "A Eurasian Union No More?" *National Interest*, April 23, 2014. As of January 23, 2017:
http://nationalinterest.org/feature/eurasian-union-no-more-10296

Berezkin, G. A. "Lessons and Conclusions from the War in Iraq," *Voyennaya Mysl [Military Thought]*, July 11, 2003.

Bezrukov, Andrei, and Andrei Sushentsov, "Contours of an Alarming Future," *Russia in Global Affairs*, No. 3, September 2015. As of January 23, 2017:
http://eng.globalaffairs.ru/number/Contours-of-an-Alarming-Future-17693

Bildt, Carl, *Russia, the European Union, and the Eastern Partnership*, European Council on Foreign Relations, May 19, 2015. As of January 23, 2017:
http://www.ecfr.eu/page/-/Riga_papers_Carl_Bildt.pdf

Blome, Nikolaus, Kai Diekmann, and Daniel Biskup, "Putin—The Interview: 'For Me, It Is Not Borders That Matter,'" *Bild*, January 11, 2016. As of January 23, 2017:
http://www.bild.de/politik/ausland/wladimir-putin/
russian-president-vladimir-putin-the-interview-44104378.bild.html

Bodner, Matthew, "With Ukraine Revitalizing NATO, Russia Dusts Off Its Own Security Alliance," *Moscow Times*, October 23, 2014. As of January 23, 2017:
http://www.themoscowtimes.com/business/article/
with-ukraine-revitalizing-nato-russia-dusts-off-its-own-security-alliance/
509986.html

Boghani, Priyanka, "New Russia Bill Targets 'Undesirable' Foreign Organizations," PBS Frontline, January 21, 2015. As of January 23, 2017:
http://www.pbs.org/wgbh/frontline/article/
new-russia-bill-targets-undesirable-foreign-organizations/

Brezinski, Ian, *Ukrainian Reforms Two Years After the Maidan Revolution and the Russian Invasion*, Testimony Before the Senate Committee on Foreign Relations, Washington, D.C.: Government Printing Office, March 15, 2016. As of January 23, 2017:
http://www.foreign.senate.gov/imo/media/doc/031516_Brzezinski_Testimony.pdf

Brzezinski, Zbigniew, and Paige Sullivan, eds., *Russia and the Commonwealth of Independent States: Documents, Data, and Analysis*, Armonk, N.Y.: M.E. Sharpe, 1997.

Burns, Robert, "Carter Says Russia, China Potentially Threaten Global Order," *Military.com*, November 8, 2015. As of January 23, 2017:
http://www.military.com/daily-news/2015/11/08/
russia-and-china-potentially-threaten-global-order-carter-says.html

Centre for the Study of Public Policy at the University of Strathclyde, "Final Result of the Duma Election, 4 December 2011," Moscow: The Levada Center, August 12, 2015. As of January 23, 2017:
http://www.russiavotes.org/duma/duma_today.php

Charap, Samuel, and Jeremy Shapiro, "US-Russian Relations: The Middle Cannot Hold," *Bulletin of the Atomic Scientist*, Vol. 72, No. 3, April 14, 2016, pp. 150–155.

Chivvis, Christopher, *Toppling Qaddafi: Libya and the Limits of Liberal Intervention*, New York: Cambridge University Press, 2014.

———, "Time to Bury Plans for Counter-Terrorism Cooperation with Russia in Syria," *National Interest*, September 23, 2016. As of January 23, 2017:
http://nationalinterest.org/blog/the-buzz/
time-bury-plans-counter-terrorism-cooperation-russia-syria-17823

Coalson, Robert, "Top Russian General Lays Bare Putin's Plan for Ukraine," *Huffington Post*, November 2, 2014. As of January 23, 2017:
http://www.huffingtonpost.com/robert-coalson/
valery-gerasimov-putin-ukraine_b_5748480.html

Commission on Security and Cooperation in Europe, *The Human Dimension*, Washington, D.C., 1991. As of January 23, 2017:
http://csce.gov/index.cfm?FuseAction=AboutCommission.HumanDimensionOf
HelsinkiProcess&IsTextOnly=True

"Commonwealth of Independent States: Charter," *International Legal Materials*, Vol. 34, No. 5, September 1995, pp. 1279–1297.

Conley, Heather, James Mina, Ruslan Stefanov, and Martin Vladimirov, *The Kremlin Playbook: Understanding Russian Influence in Central and Eastern Europe*, Center for Strategic and International Studies, October 2016. As of January 23, 2017:
https://csis-prod.s3.amazonaws.com/s3fs-public/publication/
1601017_Conley_KremlinPlaybook_Web.pdf

Connolly, Richard, and Philip Hanson, "Import Substitution and Economic Sovereignty in Russia," Chatham House, June 2016.

Crane, Keith, Shathi Nataraj, Patrick Johnston, and Gursel Rafig oglu Aliyev, *Russia's Medium-Term Economic Prospects*, Santa Monica, Calif.: RAND Corporation, RR-1468-RC, 2016. As of January 23, 2017: http://www.rand.org/pubs/research_reports/RR1468.html

CSCE—*See* Commission on Security and Cooperation in Europe.

Dannreuther, Roland, *Russian Perceptions of the Atlantic Alliance*, Edinburgh, Scotland: Edinburgh University, 1997. As of January 23, 2017: http://www.nato.int/acad/fellow/95-97/dannreut.pdf

Darczewska, Jolanta, *The Anatomy of Russian Information Warfare: The Crimean Operation—A Case Study*, Warsaw: Centre for Eastern Studies (OSW), May 2014.

Dawisha, Karen, *Putin's Kleptocracy: Who Owns Russia?* New York: Simon & Schuster, 2014.

"Declaration of Heads of Member States of SCO," Astana, Kazakhstan, *China Daily*, July 5, 2005. As of October 28, 2016: http://www.chinadaily.com.cn/china/2006-06/12/content_6020345.htm

"Declassified Cable: Memorandum of Conversation Between James A. Baker, Mikhail Gorbachev, and Eduard Shevardnadze at the Kremlin," Washington, D.C.: U.S. Department of State, February 9, 1990.

Dal Santo, Matthew, "Russia's Success in Syria Signals an Emerging Multipolar World Order," *Lowy Interpreter*, April 6, 2016. As of January 23, 2017: http://www.lowyinterpreter.org/post/2016/04/06/ Russias-success-in-Syria-signals-an-emerging-multipolar-world-order.aspx

Dibb, Paul, "Why Russia Is a Threat to the International Order," *The Strategist*, Australian Strategic Policy Institute, June 29, 2016. As of January 23, 2017: http://www.aspistrategist.org.au/russia-threat-international-order

Dragneva, Rilka, and Joop De Kort, "The Legal Regime for Free Trade in the Commonwealth of Independent States," *International and Comparative Law Quarterly*, Vol. 56, No. 2, April 2007, pp. 233–266.

Dragneva, Rilka, and Kataryna Wolczuk, *Russia, the Eurasian Customs Union and the EU: Cooperation, Stagnation or Rivalry?* London: Chatham House, August 2012.

Dugin, Aleksandr, "The Eurasist Vision: Basic Principles of the Eurasist Doctrinal Platform," *The Fourth Political Theory*, undated. As of January 23, 2017: http://www.4pt.su/en/content/eurasist-vision

———, "The Great War of Continents," in *Konspirologiya* [*Conspirology*], Moscow: Arctogeya, 1993. As of January 23, 2017: http://www.amerika.org/texts/the-great-war-of-continents-aleksandr-dugin/

———, "Eurasia Above All: Manifesto of the Eurasist Movement," trans. M. Conserva, *Arctogaia*, January 1, 2001. As of January 23, 2017: http://arctogaia.com/public/eng/Manifesto.html

———, "Eurasian Keys to the Future," *The Fourth Political Theory*, May 2012. As of January 23, 2017: http://4pt.su/en/content/eurasian-keys-future

Dunlop, John B., "Aleksandr Dugin's *Foundations of Geopolitics*," *Demokratizatsiya*, Vol. 12, No. 1, January 31, 2004.

Dvorkin, Vladimir, "Wars and Armies: Carte Blanche: A New Treaty of the Extension of START III," *Nezavisimaya Gazeta Online*, August 23, 2016.

Fean, Dominic, *Decoding Russia's WTO Accession*, Institut Français des Relations Internationales Russia/NIS Center, February 2012. As of January 23, 2017: https://www.ifri.org/sites/default/files/atoms/files/ifrifeanrussiawtoengfeb2012.pdf

Fitzpatrick, Catherine, "Russia This Week: Dugin Dismissed from Moscow State University?" *Interpreter Magazine*, June 24, 2014. As of January 23, 2017: http://www.interpretermag.com/russia-this-week-what-will-be-twitters-fate-in-russia/

Gaddy, Clifford G., and Barry W. Ickes, "Putin's Rent Management System and the Future of Addiction in Russia," in Susanne Oxenstierna, ed., *The Challenges of Russia's Politicized Economic System*, Abingdon, Oxon, UK: Routledge, 2015, pp. 11–32.

Gardner, Andrew, "Armenia Chooses Russia over EU," *Politico*, September 3, 2013. As of January 23, 2017: http://www.politico.eu/article/armenia-chooses-russia-over-eu/

Gerasimov, Valeriy, "Tsennost' Nauki v Predvidenii [The Value of Science in Foresight]," *Voenno-Promyshlennyj Kuryer* [Military-Industrial Courier], February 27, 2013. As of March 27, 2017: http://vpk-news.ru/articles/14632

———, "Po Opytu Sirii [According to the Experience of Syria]," *Voennoe Promyshlennoe Kuryer* [*Military Industrial Courier*], March 9, 2016. As of January 23, 2017: http://vpk-news.ru/articles/29579

Gordon, Michael R., "U.S. Says Russia Failed to Correct Violation of Landmark 1987 Arms Control Deal," *New York Times*, June 5, 2015. As of January 23, 2017: http://www.nytimes.com/2015/06/06/world/europe/us-says-russia-fails-to-correct-violation-of-landmark-1987-arms-control-deal.html

Gorenburg, Dmitry, *Countering Color Revolutions: Russia's New Security Strategy and Its Implications for U.S. Policy*, PONARS Eurasia, Memo 342, September 2014. As of January 23, 2017:
http://www.ponarseurasia.org/memo/countering-color-revolutions-russia's-new-security-strategy-and-its-implications-us-policy

———, "Moscow Conference on International Security 2015 Part 2: Gerasimov on Military Threats Facing Russia," Russian Military Reform blog, Cambridge, Mass., May 4, 2015. As of January 23, 2017:
https://russiamil.wordpress.com/2015/05/04/moscow-conference-on-international-security-2015-part-2-gerasimov-on-military-threats-facing-russia/

Gudkov, Dmitri, "Osoboe Mnenie [Unique Perspective]," trans. Clinton Reach, *Echo of Moscow*, November 19, 2015. As of January 23, 2017:
http://echo.msk.ru/programs/personalno/1661058-echo/

Gutterman, Steve, "Putin Says Russia Seeking IMF Reform, Battling Offshores," Reuters, June 13, 2013. As of January 23, 2017:
http://www.reuters.com/article/us-g8-russia-putin-idUSBRE95C18N20130613

Herszenhorn, David M., "Russia Quickly Maneuvers to Capitalize on Iran Nuclear Deal," *New York Times*, July 14, 2015. As of January 23, 2017:
https://www.nytimes.com/2015/07/15/world/europe/russia-quickly-maneuvers-to-capitalize-on-iran-nuclear-deal.html

Hill, Fiona, "Putin: The One-Man Show the West Doesn't Understand," *Bulletin of the Atomic Scientists*, Vol. 72, No. 3, 2016, pp. 140–144.

Hill, Fiona, and Clifford Gaddy, *Mr. Putin: Operative in the Kremlin*, Washington, D.C.: Brookings Institution Press, 2013.

Hoffman, David, "Putin on Joining NATO: 'If as Equals, Why Not?'" *Moscow Times*, March 7, 2000. As of January 23, 2017:
http://old.themoscowtimes.com/sitemap/free/2000/3/article/putin-on-joining-nato-if-as-equals-why-not/265846.html

Holbrooke, Richard, *To End a War: The Conflict in Yugoslavia—America's Inside Story—Negotiating with Milosevic*, New York: Modern Library, 1999.

Huntington, Samuel, "The Clash of Civilizations?" *Foreign Affairs*, Summer 1993. As of January 23, 2017:
https://www.foreignaffairs.com/articles/united-states/1993-06-01/clash-civilizations

International Institute for Strategic Studies, *The Military Balance*, New York: Taylor & Francis Group, March 14, 2013.

Ivanov, Igor, and Madeleine K. Albright, "Joint Press Conference," Moscow, January 26, 1999. As of January 23, 2017:
http://1997-2001.state.gov/www/statements/1999/990126a.html

Ivanov, Sergey, "Don't Think the Kremlin Always Decides Everything, Sometimes It Doesn't," TASS Russian News Agency, October 19, 2015. As of January 23, 2017:
http://tass.ru/en/politics/829778

Johnson, A. Ross, "History," Radio Free Europe/Radio Liberty, December 2008. As of January 23, 2017:
https://pressroom.rferl.org/p/6092.html

Kennan, George, "The Charge in the Soviet Union (Kennan) to the Secretary of State," telegram to James F. Byrnes, Moscow, 1946. As of January 23, 2017:
http://nsarchive.gwu.edu/coldwar/documents/episode-1/kennan.htm

——— (originally published as "X"), "The Sources of Soviet Conduct," *Foreign Affairs*, July 1947. As of January 23, 2017:
https://www.foreignaffairs.com/articles/russian-federation/1947-07-01/sources-soviet-conduct

Kissinger, Henry A., "Russia a Partner, but Not in NATO," *Washington Post*, December 7, 2001. As of January 23, 2017:
https://www.washingtonpost.com/archive/opinions/2001/12/07/russia-a-partner-but-not-in-nato/b61cd02f-7d7f-43e8-ae76-2f06e50e2fa2/

Kotkin, Stephen, "Russia's Perpetual Geopolitics: Putin Returns to Historical Patterns," *Foreign Affairs*, May/June 2016. As of January 23, 2017:
https://www.foreignaffairs.com/articles/ukraine/2016-04-18/russias-perpetual-geopolitics

Kramer, Mark, "The Myth of a No-NATO-Enlargement Pledge to Russia," *Washington Quarterly*, Vol. 32, No. 2, April 2009, pp. 39–61.

Krastev, Ivan, "Why Putin Loves Trump," *New York Times*, January 12, 2016. As of January 23, 2017:
http://www.nytimes.com/2016/01/13/opinion/why-putin-loves-trump.html

Kuchins, Andrew, and Igor Zevelev, "Russian Foreign Policy: Continuity in Change," *Washington Quarterly*, Vol. 35, No. 1, Winter 2012.

Kudrin, Alexey, and Evsey Gurvich, "A New Growth Model for the Russian Economy," *Russian Journal of Economics*, Vol. 1, 2015, pp. 30–54.

Kulikova, Alexandra, "China-Russia Cyber-Security Pact: Should the US Be Concerned?" *Russia Direct*, May 21, 2015. As of January 23, 2017:
http://www.russia-direct.org/analysis/china-russia-cyber-security-pact-should-us-be-concerned

Kuzmin, Eduard, "Interview: In Order to Protect National Dignity, Russia Is Prepared to Use Even Nuclear Weapons," *Jutarnji List*, April 17, 1999.

Laruelle, Marlène, *Russian Eurasianism: Ideology of Empire*, Washington, D.C.: Woodrow Wilson Center Press, 2012.

————, *The "Russian World": Russia's Soft Power and Geopolitical Imagination*, Washington, D.C.: Center on Global Interests, May 2015.

Lascurettes, Kyle, *The Concert of Europe and Great-Power Governance Today: What Can the Order of 19th-Century Europe Teach Policymakers About International Order in the 21st Century?* Santa Monica, Calif.: RAND Corporation, PE-226-OSD, 2017. As of February 3, 2017: http://www.rand.org/pubs/perspectives/PE226.html

Lavrov, Sergey, "The Euro-Atlantic Region: Equal Security for All," *Russia in Global Affairs*, July 7, 2010. As of January 23, 2017: http://eng.globalaffairs.ru/number/ The_Euro-Atlantic_Region:_Equal_Security_for_All-14888

————, "Russia's Foreign Policy: Historical Background," *Russia in Global Affairs*, March 5, 2016. As of January 23, 2017: http://www.voltairenet.org/article190623.html

Lukin, Alexander, "Russia in a Post-Bipolar World," *Survival: Global Politics and Strategy*, Vol. 58, No. 1, February–March 2016.

Lukyanov, Fyodor, "The World in 2015: A Nostalgia for Balance," *Russia in Global Affairs*, December 24, 2015. As of January 23, 2017: http://eng.globalaffairs.ru/redcol/The-world-in-2015-A-nostalgia-for-balance-17905

————, "The Lost Twenty-Five Years," *Russia in Global Affairs*, February 28, 2016a. As of January 23, 2017: http://eng.globalaffairs.ru/redcol/The-Lost-Twenty-Five-Years-18012

————, "Putin's Foreign Policy," *Foreign Affairs*, May/June 2016b.

Mankoff, Jeffery, *Russian Foreign Policy: The Return of Great Power Politics*, Lanham, Md.: Rowman & Littlefield Publishers, 2009.

Mardell, Mark, "What Syria Reveals About the New World Order," BBC, October 3, 2016. As of January 23, 2017: http://www.bbc.com/news/world-middle-east-37512095

Maruyev, A. Yu, "Russia and the U.S.A. in Confrontation: Military and Political Aspects," *Military Thought*, July 1, 2009–September 30 2009.

Mazarr, Michael, Miranda Priebe, Andrew Radin, and Astrid Stuth Cevallos, *Understanding the Current International Order*, RAND Corporation, RR-1598-OSD, 2016. As of January 23, 2017: http://www.rand.org/pubs/research_reports/RR1598.html

McCausland, Jeffrey D., "NATO and Russian Approaches to Adapting the CFE Treaty," *Arms Control Association*, August 1, 1997. As of January 23, 2017: http://www.armscontrol.org/print/232

McFaul, Michael, Stephen Sestanovich, and John J. Mearsheimer, "Faulty Powers: Who Started the Ukraine Crisis?" *Foreign Affairs*, November/December 2014. As of January 23, 2017:
https://www.foreignaffairs.com/articles/eastern-europe-caucasus/2014-10-17/faulty-powers

Mearsheimer, John J., *The Tragedy of Great Power Politics*, New York: W. W. Norton, 2001.

———, "Why the Ukraine Crisis Is the West's Fault: The Liberal Delusions That Provoked Putin," *Foreign Affairs*, September/October 2014. As of January 23, 2017:
https://www.foreignaffairs.com/articles/russia-fsu/2014-08-18/why-ukraine-crisis-west-s-fault

"Medvedev: Blocking Russia's WTO Entry," CNN, September 15, 2009. As of January 23, 2017:
http://www.cnn.com/2009/WORLD/europe/09/15/russia.us.wto/index.html?iref=nextin

Ministry of Foreign Affairs of the Russian Federation, *Conception of the Foreign Policy of the Russian Federation*, 1993.

———, *Information Security Doctrine of the Russian Federation*, December 29, 2008.

———, *Convention on International Information Security*, September 22, 2011. As of January 23, 2017:
http://www.mid.ru/en/foreign_policy/official_documents/-/asset_publisher/CptICkB6BZ29/content/id/191666

———, *Concept of the Foreign Policy of the Russian Federation*, February 12, 2013. As of January 23, 2017:
http://www.mid.ru/en/foreign_policy/official_documents/-/asset_publisher/CptICkB6BZ29/content/id/122186

———, "Foreign Minister Sergey Lavrov's Interview with Venezuelan State Television," October 2, 2015. As of January 23, 2017:
http://www.mid.ru/en_GB/foreign_policy/news/-/asset_publisher/cKNonkJE02Bw/content/id/1825673

Mowchan, John, *The Militarization of the Collective Security Treaty Organization*, Carlisle, Penn.: Center for Strategic Leadership, U.S. Army War College, Issue Paper, Vol. 6-09, July 2009. As of January 23, 2017:
http://www.csl.army.mil/usacsl/publications/IP_6_09_Militarization_of_the_CSTO.pdf

Mukhin, Vladimir, "Moscow Adjusts Military Doctrine: Events in Ukraine Are Making Russia Amend Documents Defining National Security Strategy," *Nezavisimaya Gazeta*, August 1, 2014.

NATO—See North Atlantic Treaty Organization.

Nichols, Michelle, and Yara Bayoumy, "U.S. Slams Russian 'Barbarism' in Syria," Reuters, September 25, 2016. As of January 23, 2017: http://www.reuters.com/article/us-mideast-crisis-syria-un-us-idUSKCN11V0NN

North Atlantic Treaty Organization, "Founding Act on Mutual Relations, Cooperation and Security Between NATO and the Russian Federation, Signed in Paris, France," May 27, 1997. As of January 23, 2017: http://www.nato.int/cps/en/natohq/official_texts_25468.htm

———, "Bucharest Summit Declaration," April 3, 2008. As of January 23, 2017: http://www.nato.int/cps/en/natolive/official_texts_8443.htm

Oliker, Olga, Keith Crane, Lowell H. Schwartz, and Catherine Yusupov, *Russian Foreign Policy: Sources and Implications*, Santa Monica, Calif.: RAND Corporation, MG-768-A, 2009. As of January 23, 2017: http://www.rand.org/pubs/monographs/MG768.html

Paderin, A. A., "Policy and Military Strategy: A Unity Lesson," *Military Thought*, April 1, 2006–June 30, 2006.

Pavlovsky, Gleb, "Putin's World Outlook," *New Left Review*, Vol. 88, July/August 2014. As of January 23, 2017: https://newleftreview.org/II/88/gleb-pavlovsky-putin-s-world-outlook

Pelnens, Gatis, ed., *The "Humanitarian Dimension" of Russian Foreign Policy Towards Georgia, Moldova, Ukraine, and the Baltic States*, Riga: Centre for East European Policy Studies, International Centre for Defence Studies, Centre for Geopolitical Studies, School for Policy Analysis at the National University of Kyiv-Mohyla Academy, Foreign Policy Association of Moldova, and International Centre for Geopolitical Studies, 2009. As of January 23, 2017: https://www.academia.edu/1376506/ The_Humanitarian_Dimension_of_Russian_Foreign_Policy_Toward._Georgia_ Moldova_Ukraine_and_the_Baltic_States

People's Freedom Party/Parnas, "Platforma Demokraticheskoy Koalitsii Parnas [Platform of the Democratic Coalition of Parnas]," Moscow, July 5, 2015. As of January 23, 2017: https://parnasparty.ru/news/42

Perry, Tom, and Jeff Mason, "Obama Urges Russia to Stop Bombing 'Moderate' Syria Rebels," Reuters, February 14, 2016. As of January 23, 2017: http://www.reuters.com/article/mideast-crisis-syria-idUSKCN0VN0M7

Pipes, Richard, *Russian Conservatism and Its Critics*, New Haven, Conn.: Yale University Press, June 28, 2007.

Prokofyev, I., V. Kholodkov, and N. Troshin, "East vs. West: Battle for Reforming the World Economy," *Russian Institute for Strategic Studies*, No. 6, January 2015.

Putin, Vladimir, "Speech in the Bundestag of the Federal Republic of Germany," Berlin: President of Russia, September 25, 2001. As of January 23, 2017:
http://en.kremlin.ru/events/president/transcripts/21340

———, "Annual Address to the Federal Assembly of the Russian Federation," Moscow, April 25, 2005. As of January 23, 2017:
http://en.kremlin.ru/events/president/transcripts/22931

———, "Putin's Prepared Remarks at 43rd Munich Conference on Security Policy," Munich, February 12, 2007. As of January 23, 2017:
http://www.washingtonpost.com/wp-dyn/content/article/2007/02/12/AR2007021200555.html

———, "Novyj Integratsionnyj Proyekt Dlya Evrazii: Budushchee, Kotoroe Rozhdaetsya Segodnya [New Integration Project for Eurasia: The Future in the Making]," *Izvestia*, October 3, 2011. As of March 27, 2017:
http://izvestia.ru/news/502761

———, "Russia and the Changing World," RT News, February 27, 2012. As of January 23, 2017:
https://www.rt.com/politics/official-word/putin-russia-changing-world-263/

———, "Address by the President of the Russian Federation," March 18, 2014a. As of January 23, 2017:
http://en.kremlin.ru/events/president/news/20603

———, "Meeting of the Valdai International Discussion Club," Sochi, Russia: Valdai International Discussion Club, October 24, 2014b. As of January 23, 2017:
http://en.kremlin.ru/events/president/news/46860

———, "Meeting of the Valdai International Discussion Club," Sochi, Russia: Valdai International Discussion Club, October 22, 2015a.

———, "Interview on Miroporyadok [World Order]," trans. Clinton Reach, Moscow: Rossiya HD, December 20, 2015b. As of January 23, 2017:
https://www.youtube.com/watch?v=ZNhYzYUo42g

"The Reform of the Administration of the President of the Russian Federation," trans. Petr Podkopaev, Karen Dawisha, and James Nealy, *Kommersant*, May 5, 2000. As of January 23, 2017:
http://miamioh.edu/cas/_files/documents/havighurst/english-putin-reform-admin.pdf

Reynolds, Paul, "New Russian World Order: The Five Principles," BBC News, 2008. As of January 23, 2017:
http://news.bbc.co.uk/2/hi/europe/7591610.stm

Rivera, Sharon Werning, James Bryan, Brisa Camacho-Lovell, Carlos Fineman, Nora Klemmer, and Emma Raynor, *2016 Hamilton College Levitt Poll: The Russian Elite 2016—Perspectives on Foreign Policy and Domestic Policy*, Clinton, N.Y.: Hamilton College, Arthur Levitt Public Affairs Center, May 11, 2016. As of January 23, 2017:
https://www.hamilton.edu/documents/russianelite2016final1.pdf

"Russia Becomes 3rd-Biggest Shareholder in China-Led Development Bank," *Moscow Times*, June 29, 2015. As of January 23, 2017:
http://www.themoscowtimes.com/business/article/
russia-becomes-3rd-biggest-shareholder-in-china-led-development-bank/
524587.html

Russian Federation, *National Security Strategy of the Russian Federation to 2020*, May 12, 2009.

———, *National Security Strategy*, December 31, 2015.

———, "Miroporyadok [World Order]," documentary, December 2015. As of January 23, 2017:
https://www.youtube.com/watch?v=ZNhYzYUo42g

Russian Presidency of the 2015 Ufa Summit, "VII BRICS Summit: 2015 Ufa Declaration," University of Toronto BRICS Information Center, July 9, 2015. As of January 23, 2017:
http://www.brics.utoronto.ca/docs/150709-ufa-declaration_en.html

Saivetz, Carol R., "The Ties That Bind? Russia's Evolving Relations with Its Neighbors," *Communist and Post-Communist Studies*, Vol. 45, No. 3–4, 2012, pp. 401–412.

Schenkkan, Nate, "Eurasian Disunion: Why the Union Might Not Survive 2015," *Foreign Affairs*, December 26, 2014. As of January 23, 2017:
https://www.foreignaffairs.com/articles/armenia/2014-12-26/eurasian-disunion

Shlapak, David, and Michael Johnson, *Reinforcing Deterrence on NATO's Eastern Flank: Wargaming the Defense of the Baltics*, Santa Monica, Calif.: RAND Corporation, RR-1253-A, 2016. As of January 23, 2017:
http://www.rand.org/pubs/research_reports/RR1253.html

Shevtsova, Lilia, *Russia: Lost in Transition*, Washington, D.C.: Carnegie Endowment for International Peace, 2007.

———, "How the West Misjudged Russia, Parts 1–13," *American Interest*, 2016. As of January 23, 2017:
http://www.the-american-interest.com/byline/shevtsova/

Shifrinson, Joshua Itzkowitz, "Deal or No Deal? The End of the Cold War and the U.S. Offer to Limit NATO Expansion," *International Security*, Vol. 40, No. 4, Spring 2016, pp. 7–44.

Shuster, Simon, "Why Russia Is Rebuilding Its Nuclear Arsenal," *Time*, April 4, 2016. As of January 23, 2017:
http://time.com/4280169/russia-nuclear-security-summit/

Sonne, Paul, "U.S. Is Trying to Dismember Russia, Says Putin Adviser," *Wall Street Journal*, February 11, 2015. As of January 23, 2017:
http://www.wsj.com/articles/
u-s-is-trying-to-dismember-russia-says-putin-adviser-1423667319

Stent, Angela, *The Limits of Partnership: U.S.-Russian Relations in the Twenty-First Century*, Princeton, N.J.: Princeton University Press, 2014.

———, "Putin's Power Play in Syria: How to Respond to Russia's Intervention," *Foreign Affairs*, January/February 2016. As of January 23, 2017:
https://www.foreignaffairs.com/articles/united-states/2015-12-14/
putins-power-play-syria

"Summit of Failure: How the EU Lost Russia over Ukraine," Spiegel International, October 16, 2014. As of January 23, 2017:
http://www.spiegel.de/international/europe/war-in-ukraine-a-result-of-
misunderstandings-between-europe-and-russia-a-1004706-2.html

Suny, Ronald Grigor, *The Empire Strikes Out: Imperial Russia, "National" Identity, and Theories of Empire*, Chicago: University of Chicago Press, 1997. As of January 23, 2017:
http://www.dartmouth.edu/~crn/crn_papers/Suny4.pdf

Suslov, Dmitry, "'Normandy Four': The Best Possible Format," Valdai International Discussion Club, February 10, 2015. As of January 23, 2017:
http://valdaiclub.com/opinion/highlights/normandy-four-the-best-possible-format/

"Syria Conflict: US-Russia Brokered Truce to Start at Weekend," BBC News, February 22, 2016. As of January 23, 2017:
http://www.bbc.com/news/world-middle-east-35634695

"Syria Crisis: Putin 'Confident' on Chemical Weapons Plan," BBC News, September 19, 2013. As of January 23, 2017:
http://www.bbc.com/news/world-middle-east-24166891

Tagliabue, John, "France and Russia Ready to Use Veto Against Iraq War," *New York Times*, March 6, 2003. As of January 23, 2017:
http://www.nytimes.com/2003/03/06/international/europe/
06IRAQ.html?pagewanted=1

Talbott, Strobe, *The Russia Hand: A Memoir of Presidential Diplomacy*, New York: Random House, 2002.

Tashlykov, S. L., "General and Particular Features of Present-Day Conflicts Involving the U.S. and Its Allies," *Military Thought*, July 1, 2010–September 30, 2010.

Tran, Mark, "Russia Will Pursue Chechnya Campaign Says Yeltsin," *The Guardian*, November 15, 1999. As of January 23, 2017:
http://www.theguardian.com/world/1999/nov/15/chechnya.marktran

Treisman, Daniel, "Why Putin Took Crimea," *Foreign Affairs*, May/June 2016, pp. 48–54.

Trenin, Dmitri, *The End of Eurasia: Russia on the Border Between Geopolitics and Globalization*, Washington, D.C.: Carnegie Endowment for International Peace, 2001.

———, "Russia Leaves the West," *Foreign Affairs*, July/August 2006.

———, "NATO and Russia: Sobering Thoughts and Practical Suggestions," *NATO Review*, Summer 2007. As of January 23, 2017:
http://www.nato.int/docu/review/2007/issue2/english/art1.html

———, *Post-Imperium: A Eurasian Story*, Washington, D.C.: Carnegie Endowment for International Peace, 2011.

———, *Russia's Breakout from the Post–Cold War System: The Drivers of Putin's Course*, Moscow: Carnegie Moscow Center, December 2014.

Tsygankov, Andrei P., "Preserving Influence in a Changing World," *Problems of Post-Communism*, Vol. 58, No. 2, 2011, pp. 28–54.

"Two Years On: How Russia's Agricultural Sector Reaps the Benefits of Sanctions," *Sputnik News*, August 7, 2016. As of January 23, 2017:
https://sputniknews.com/russia/201608071044026162-russia-counter-sanctions-two-years/

United Nations, United Nations Bibliographic Information System, undated. As of January 23, 2017:
http://unbisnet.un.org

UK Foreign and Commonwealth Office, "Response to General Assembly Resolution 69/28: 'Developments in the Field of Information and Telecommunications in the Context of International Security,'" May 2015. As of January 23, 2017:
https://unoda-web.s3.amazonaws.com/wp-content/uploads/2015/08/UKISinfull.pdf

U.S. Army Special Operations Command, *"Little Green Men": A Primer on Modern Russian Unconventional Warfare, Ukraine 2013–2014*, Fort Bragg, N.C., undated. As of January 23, 2017:
http://www.jhuapl.edu/ourwork/nsa/papers/ARIS_LittleGreenMen.pdf

U.S. Department of State, "Joint Press Statement for the 2015 U.S.-European Union Information Society Dialogue," Washington, D.C., April 2015. As of January 23, 2017:
https://www.highbeam.com/doc/1G1-409626044.html

U.S. Mission to NATO, "Why NATO Matters," Brussels, undated. As of January 23, 2017:
https://nato.usmission.gov/our-relationship/why-nato-matters/

Weitz, Richard, *The Rise and Fall of Medvedev's European Security Treaty*, Washington, D.C.: German Marshall Fund of the United States, May 2012. As of January 23, 2017:
http://www.hudson.org/content/researchattachments/attachment/1037/1338307624weitz_medvedevsest_may12.pdf

White House, *National Security Strategy*, February 2015. As of January 23, 2017:
https://obamawhitehouse.archives.gov/sites/default/files/docs/2015_national_security_strategy_2.pdf

Woolf, Amy F., Paul K. Kerr, and Mary Beth D. Nikitin, *Arms Control and Nonproliferation: A Catalog of Treaties and Agreements*, Washington, D.C.: Congressional Research Service, RL33865, April 13, 2016.

Yabloko Political Committee, "Operation in Syria and the Threats to the National Security," Moscow: Russian United Democratic Party Yabloko, November 16, 2015. As of January 23, 2017:
http://eng.yabloko.ru/?p=10680

"Yeltsin Warns of Possible World War over Kosovo," CNN, April 9, 1999. As of January 23, 2017:
http://www.cnn.com/WORLD/europe/9904/09/kosovo.diplomacy.02/

"Yeltsin: West Has 'No Right' to Criticize Chechen Campaign," CNN, November 18, 1999. As of January 23, 2017:
http://www.cnn.com/WORLD/europe/9911/18/osce.summit/

Zellner, Wolfgang, "Russia and the OSCE: From High Hopes to Disillusionment," *Cambridge Review of International Affairs*, Vol. 18, No. 3, 2005, pp. 389–402.

Zevelev, Igor, *NATO's Enlargement and Russian Perceptions of Eurasian Political Frontiers*, Garmisch-Partenkirchen, Germany: George Marshall European Center for Security Studies, undated. As of January 23, 2017:
http://www.nato.int/acad/fellow/98-00/zevelev.pdf

———, "The Russian World Boundaries: Russia's National Identity Transformation and New Foreign Policy Doctrine," *Russia in Global Affairs*, June 7, 2014. As of January 23, 2017:
http://eng.globalaffairs.ru/number/The-Russian-World-Boundaries-16707

Zimmerman, William, Ronald Inglehart, Eduard Ponarin, Yegor Lazarev, Boris Sokolov, Irina Vartanova, and Yekaterina Turanova, *Russian Elite—2020: Valdai Discussion Club Grantees Analytic Report*, Moscow: Valdai International Discussion Club, July 2013. As of January 23, 2017:
http://vid-1.rian.ru/ig/valdai/Russian_elite_2020_eng.pdf